THE PERFECT...

FOOD NOTES AND RECIPES

RICHARD EHRLICH

Illustrations by Gillian Blease

GRUB STREET • LONDON

ACKNOWLEDGEMENTS

The only part of writing that gives me angst-free pleasure is thanking the people who have helped me. Here is the roster for this book.

I am deeply grateful to *The Guardian* for allowing me the privilege of writing the original column for nearly three years with minimal intervention. And indebted especially to three people, first of whom is Katherine Viner, editor of the *Weekend* section. She came up with the idea in the first place, then let me develop it as I saw fit. Second is Matthew Fort, editor of the Food and Drink pages, who treated me with far more kindness and respect than I deserved in the fifteen years I wrote for him. Third, and especially gratifying to thank, is chief sub-editor Bob Granleese. He handled my copy with a skill and sensitivity that preserved what was good and improved what was clumsy – while making it all fit into a difficult space. If I have lost any of his contributions by my editing for this book, the fault is mine and not his. Gillian Blease created illustrations for my column during every week of its existence. I derived immense pleasure from looking at them, and am delighted to see them find a new home in this book.

In the course of writing my column, I have made use of ideas and recipes from other cookery writers and from a number of chefs. They are cited in the relevant items so I will not name them all here, but I am grateful to all for their generosity. Two restaurants that require special mention: the Junction Tavern, London NW5, for their onion soup recipe, and Zuzu, Napa, California, for their barbecue sauce.

This book would not be in your hands without the commitment of my publisher, Anne Dolamore. She stood by patiently when I was late delivering, and then edited the manuscript with meticulous care.

As always, a debt I can never acknowledge adequately: to my mother, Norma Ehrlich, who taught me how to cook; to my father, Eugene Ehrlich, who taught me to settle for nothing less than the best, most precise word; and to both of them together, for everything.

I am grateful, finally, to my wife, Emma Dally, and my daughters, Rebecca, Alice and Ruth. Much of what you'll find in this book arose directly from the necessity of feeding all four of them. Many of my simple shortcuts to gastronomic satisfaction found their origins in the experience of cooking for my children, whose increasingly demanding palates demanded that I find new ways of taking basic ingredients and turning them into something better than basic. They are present in every page of this book. They have forced me to be a better cook. For that, and for much else, I am forever in their debt.

First published in 2004 by
Grub Street
4 Rainham Close
London
SW11 6SS
Email: food@grubstreet.co.uk
www.grubstreet.co.uk

Text copyright © Richard Ehrlich 2004
Copyright this edition © Grub Street 2004
Illustrations © Gillian Blease 2004
Book and jacket design by Hugh Adams, AB3 Design

The right of Richard Ehrlich to be identified as the author of this work has been asserted by him in accordance with the Copyright, Designs and Patents Act 1988.

A CIP catalogue record for this book is available from the British Library
ISBN 1 904010 83 0

Printed and bound in Spain by Bookprint, S.L.

CONTENTS

INTRODUCTION

This book occupies one of the riskiest of categories of cookery writing: it is a compilation of articles that originally appeared in a newspaper. The paper is *The Guardian*, and the columns were published there on a weekly basis between 2001 and early 2004. That accounts, in part, for several peculiarities that will become immediately apparent when you look through its pages. This is not a conventional cookbook in any sense.

In the column from which it arose, I was not asked to give standard recipes consisting of an ingredients list followed by a detailed method. My column aimed, instead, to get to the essence of a particular dish: the important points to remember, and the things one needs to know not just to achieve success but to avoid problems. Over nearly 150 weeks of writing it, I branched out into other types of information: simple dishes I had developed through domestic experimentation, and some dishes I adapted (or just stole) after eating them in restaurants. But even in these variations, I eschewed the conventional recipe format in favour of a descriptive, expository approach.

This approach suited me well because I have long thought that recipes can get in the way of good cooking. What matters in the kitchen is an understanding of fundamental principles, mastering essential skills, and – most important – just paying very close attention to what happens to food as you expose it to knife, mixing bowl, and finally the heat of the frying pan or the oven. In an ideal world, I would like everyone to stop using recipes as blueprints and regard them instead as starting points for their own empirical investigations. Precise adherence to prescribed measurements, cooking times, and even ingredients lists is less important than developing sound cooking sense. This ideal underlies the texts in these pages.

Nor is **The Perfect...**a comprehensive cookbook in any sense. It reflects my columns, which were never designed to add up to a full introduction to any particular area of the culinary life. But there is more to this incompleteness than the vagaries of journalistic writing. My column has always reflected my own tastes and the areas of concerted kitchen work that necessarily required my fullest attention. There are, for instance, a large number of chicken ideas here because my family and I eat a lot of chicken. There are relatively few sweet things, because we don't usually eat them except on state occasions. There are quite a few sauces and dressings because I've always found that it's easier and faster to make a simple dish of plainly cooked fish, meat or whatever and then jazz it up with something prepared separately. And there are a lot of vegetables because, though we're not vegetarians, we eat vegetables at every meal.

In a sense, therefore, my column has been shaped not by journalistic requirements but by something I share with every other home cook: the need to feed a family. I have had the privilege of turning that need into something I can share with others.

One necessary note about the inconsistent presentation of the material here. For the first year or so of my column, I wrote it to a length of 225 words. After that, the length was increased to 470 words. The shorter, earlier columns will be immediately identifiable here, and in most cases I have not expanded them greatly. They were written with great deliberation and great care. Even though the imposingly short length sometimes made my life difficult, it also presented me with the challenge of distilling my understanding of the subject at hand into very few words. I have tried to preserve that concentration of language and information in this book.

Some pieces here, however, are much longer. In some cases that's because they date from the change of length in the paper. In other cases, greater length results from inclusion of extra material that I sent out, from time to time, to *Guardian* readers via email. These extra offerings gave me the chance to expand to essentially unlimited length on a particular subject. I am delighted to be able to publish them here.

Richard Ehrlich
London

THE PERFECT...

CHICKEN STOCK

Chicken stock is one of the three or four indispensable items in the kitchen of any cook who is serious about cooking, and there are two indisputable facts about it. One: dozens of cookbooks write the perfect prescription. Two: they never agree on what constitutes perfection.

And why should they agree, when it's so charmingly easy? Fact: you can cook successful chicken stock in around 8,000 different ways as long as you follow four basic rules. One: never let the water boil. Its surface should experience nothing more violent than a gentle breaking of bubbles. Two: do not rely solely on cooked chicken. Much of the flavour's gone by the time it's been through its initial cooking. Three: if using other ingredients, don't let them dominate. Chicken stock should taste mainly of chicken. Four: use any edible part of the bird except the liver, which makes cloudy, yucky stock.

Chicken scraps are ignored by supermarkets, plentiful chez le boucher. Beg, borrow, steal or even buy a huge supply; accumulate slowly, freezing the scraps in the meantime if necessary; then make enough stock to fill the freezer. Result: you're set up in the stock market for many months. Warning: some cookbooks solemnly inform us that stock shouldn't be frozen for longer than two months. Warning: they are solemnly mistaken.

Put chicken scraps – wings, necks, backs, etc. – in a pot. Add water to cover by an inch or two, and heat till you've got a steady, gentle simmer. Continue like this for a couple of hours, or longer if it suits you. At some point, skim off the frothy scum that appears on the surface. When you find that the chicken no longer has any taste (because it's all migrated to the H_2O), strain the liquid. Get rid of the fat. You have made chicken stock. It was about as difficult as blinking.

But its pleasure-potential waxes if you add a few extras. When the pot has reached simmering point, and you have skimmed off conspicuous effusions of scum, you are ready to add the A-list aromatic accessories. Figure on an ounce or so per pound of trimmings. A-list number 1 is literally that: alliums. Garlic and/or onions, topped and tailed; peeling optional. Leeks, thoroughly cleaned. A-list number 2: parsley, celery (especially leaves), carrots added in extreme moderation, peppercorns, bay leaves, a parsimonious pinch of dried herbs. Use one or all, but don't bother freezing scraps of veg: as Jacques Pépin pithily puts it: 'After a while, you accumulate hundreds of small packages with crystallised ice around them. So one day, you look around the freezer and throw them all away.' Untouchable extras: starch, strong-tasting veg, acid.

Chicken stock always-always number 1: do not turn your back when stock is sitting on a flame that can turn the simmer into a boil. I could tell many sad stories about the results. Stock always-always number 2: comprehensive clarification and de-greasing. Stock always-always number 3: sound storage.

The easy way out is to buy cubes, and the better versions are perfectly good for many applications. This book's favourite brand: Just Bouillon, widely available.

FURTHER THOUGHTS

After making chicken stock around another 50-60 times after writing the words given above, which are basically a textbook version of the procedure, my serene meditations taught me many lessons. Here are the three important ones.

Discovery number one: it is possible to overcook chicken stock. After a few episodes of extended simmering, I noticed that the characteristic sweet smell gave way to something I can only describe as bony and rank. Conclusion: don't go heating the stuff endlessly. If you need to leave stock on the hob for periodic reheating, take it off the bone (as it were) after three hours max. Discovery two: all that stuff about careful removal of rising scum? Not strictly necessary. If you simmer stock gently, the coagulating scum will adhere to the bones on top and dry out without contaminating the liquid underneath.

Discovery three, a psycho-culinary reminder of the basics: never put stock over a high heat, even 'just for a minute to get it started.' If you do, sod's law dictates that you will forget it's there. It will boil, and be ruined. Keep that heat low from start to finish. Everything else is incidental. Sermon ended.

BEEF STOCK

Beef stock, alone among the inhabitants of the stocky world, simply doesn't taste right if you just pop the bones in water and let them cook. More is needed: a preliminary browning before the bones go in. I've never understood why, but stock made from raw beef bones never tastes quite right. Chicken, veal, fish: browning not required. Beef: do it or live in regret.

A strategic word about the roasting. Most recipes share my view, but none I've seen points out that turning on the oven just to roast beef bones is a colossal waste of money and energy. Do it only when the oven is going to be on for other reasons. The ozone layer will thank you.

Roasting begins with bones and scraps. Bones: sawn into small pieces by the butcher. Scraps: offcuts, and cheap cuts like shin or brisket. Method of acquisition: buy or beg as they become available, and freeze till you have at least 1.5kg (3lb), and preferably twice that amount. Essential note: if the bones don't have much meat on them, use a higher proportion of meat or the stock will lack depth of flavour.

Got what you need? Then spread the pieces out in a big roasting pan, in something approximating a single layer. Too deep and the bones won't brown evenly. Quarter a couple of onions and carrots, and tuck them in. Pan into oven, preheated or not, at a fairly high temperature: 220C/425F/Gas 7 is a good target.

Next step: keep a casual eye on things. You are aiming for a good overall browning, without any hint

FISH STOCK

of charring, and this requires that you turn the pieces once or twice. Total browning time: could be forty minutes, could be an hour. Just make sure no blackening takes place. When all's brown, remove the pan from the oven and remove the bones to a stockpot.

Or you can make your stock in the roasting pan. This has a couple of advantages. It cuts simmering time, lets you keep a closer eye on things, and saves on washing up. Disadvantage: you need a deep pan, and you may find it more difficult to pour out the finished stock. But wherever the stock will simmer, you first have to set the pan over a medium heat on the hob and deglaze it: add liquid and scrape the bottom of the pan to loosen coagulated juices. Liquid: water or wine. Scraping: thorough.

With deglazing done, it's time to submerge dem bones. Water to cover. Make sure the deglazed juices are in there, plus extra aromatics au choix: garlic, herbs, parsley, celery, peppercorns, etc. From here on in, it's just standard stock operation. Winter sustenance, easily acquired. And don't forget: make use of that oven while it's firing away for another purpose.

Making meat stock is a long, slow, meditative process that takes place largely unaided. Making fish stock is a different kettle of – sorry, can't think of the appropriate word here – altogether. It's quick. It requires some careful work, and a bit of attention. But it's a simple process, if you remember the crucial principles of SPS: selection, preparation, speed. Selection takes place with raw materials, bones and heads from good-quality white fish only – nothing oily like mackerel, and no salmon.

Preparation means weeding out bits that will contribute off-flavours. If you're using fish heads, cut out the gills with kitchen scissors. Scrape and wash off all traces of blood, which will ruin a fish stock faster than you can say filet de sole bonne femme. Work carefully and meticulously. Leave nothing unseemly behind. Nothing. Rinse the trimmed trimmings very well.

Finally, speed: trimmings in saucepan, water to cover, slice of onion, sprig of parsley, pinch of dried herbs. Bring to the boil quickly, skim the crud off the top, then turn down the heat and simmer gently for 30 minutes max. Remember, fish cooks quickly. The hours of simmering needed for meat stock are not just unnecessary but potentially ruinous: they could extract flavours that you don't want in your finished fluid. Skim the crud, and put the stock through muslin to clarify. Done. Ready to roll with fish soup, fish pie, sauce. SPS in action.

THE PERFECT...

HOLLANDAISE

No two cookery writers make hollandaise sauce in the same way. What some regard as crucial others barely mention. The moral? You'll figure out your own way. The unalterable rule? Hollandaise must never get more than hand-hot or it will curdle. My solution? A procedure for the novice, or the merely timid. Gather 100g cold butter, cut into chunks; 2 egg yolks; juice of just under 1/4 lemon.

All set? Then heat water in a pot that can hold the bowl without letting bowl touch water, and place another pot of cold water nearby. Whisk the yolks in a clean bowl with a tiny splash of water till they're pale and frothy. Put the eggs over the simmering water and drop in a chunk of butter. Beat till the butter melts. Add another. Beat again. Every so often, dip the bowl in cold water to tame the heat. As long as you watch the heat beadily, your sauce will not curdle.

Keep doing this until the whisk leaves thick, persistent trails. Squeeze in the lemon. Beat again till those trails reappear. Salt and pepper to taste. Result: an obscenely delicious partner for asparagus, and much else besides. Best used ASAP but holdable away from heat if you reheat with final whisking. The triumph of pragmatism over dogma.

BÉCHAMEL

White sauce (sounds better in French) gives birth to dozens of sauces, all more glam than their dowdy maman. The deal: delicately cook flour and butter for a couple of minutes to make a paste (a.k.a. roux). Turn paste into a fluid by thinning it with milk. Easy. Most methods work, as long as you observe $3\frac{1}{2}$ rules.

First: equal parts of flour and butter. My béchamel blunders have flowed from cutting calories by cutting butter. Don't. Egalité = fraternité. Rule two: respect the paste's capacity to absorb fluid. In theory you could use 2ml of paste per litre of milk, but then you'd have to cook it till next July. Ready reckoner: 15-25ml paste will satisfactorily thicken 200ml milk. Some recipes tell you to heat the milk. I use cold and just add it gradually to start with.

Third rule: low heat and lots of stirring. Béchamel needs both if you want to minimise scorches and lumps. A sieve will kill persistent offenders. And cook your béchamel for a good long time: twenty minutes as a minimum, thirty's even better. With lots and lots of stirring. A whisk is better than a wooden spoon for annihilating lumps.

Half-rule: find a way that works for you, then try something different next time. It will probably work just as well, and will remind you of a cardinal cooking rule: there is more than one way to do just about everything. Historical note: the original Béchamel was a Duc. Sounds so much better in French.

EGGS

Boiling an egg successfully means achieving two things. One: getting it done the way you want it. Two: preventing shell-crack, so you don't create bulbous albumen formations in the cooking water. Here's a technique that guarantees perfection.

Temperature of eggs: irrelevant. Size of pan: more important; the egg(s) must not be crowded or the timing will go screwy. The drill: put the egg(s) in a pan of cold water to cover by an inch. (If they float, they're none too fresh.) Boil the water as quickly as possible, then reduce to a simmer and set your timer.

Very runny eggs (coddled), perfect for Caesar Salad: 1 minute. Soft-boiled to most people's view of perfection: 2 minutes. Barely hard-boiled, yolk wet at the centre: 3 minutes. Perfect hard-boiled: 7 minutes. Over-boiled: yolks brown, whites like rubber. It's not rocket science. But you need to set that timer.

If you're making hard-boiled eggs, here is a sheller's tip: run hard-boiled eggs under cold water, then crack the shells to let air in while they cool. Makes peeling a doddle (most of the time, anyway).

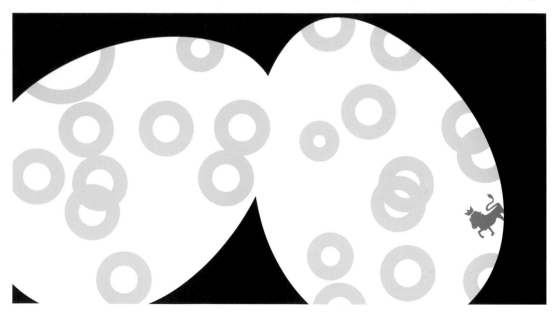

POACHING

The best method for poaching an egg is the one you've been using for thirty-seven years. You know: deep water/shallow water, vinegar/no vinegar, salt/no salt, swirling the water or not swirling. In short, there are several poaching plans. If you don't have one, however, here's my preferred method. Around 5cm (2 in) of water in a small, thick-bottomed frying pan. A teacup (or serving spoon or ladle) large enough to hold a raw egg. And, most important by far, a really fresh egg. If your egg is not fresh, the white will spread out like a carpet on the bottom of the pan, rather than staying close to the yolk like a cushion.

My preferred cooking method: get the water boiling, then turn it down so that the water barely moves. Forget 'tiny bubbles' – the ideal is no bubbles at all. Crack the egg into the cup/spoon/ladle, place the bowl on the water so it's partially submerged, and tip out the egg as gently as you can. Cook like that for around three minutes. Slotted spoon to remove.

Once you've done this a few times, you will have the confidence to poach more than one egg at a time. It's a matter of experience, like all cooking. And of having a really fresh egg.

SCRAMBLING

Scrambled eggs. A mound of soft, creamy luxury steaming in front of you on the breakfast plate. Nirvana. The way to reach it: CMS. Cool, Movement, Slow.

Cool is for your cooking vessel, a thick-bottomed

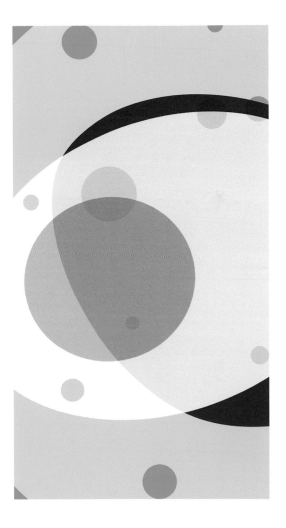

pot or pan (non-stick is best) of suitable size. Heat it over a low temperature: the butter, when added, should take a good few seconds to melt. Put in the beaten eggs – milk unnecessary – and put the M-word into action. The eggs should be kept moving constantly so you don't get large, dry curds. Cut up nascent curds with spoon or spatula. Do not stop stirring. Do not leave the pot's side.

With C and M in operation, the S word follows as surely as thunder follows lightning. Successful scrambling means slow scrambling. It can take five minutes, ten minutes, much more if you're cooking for a crowd. Those minutes are among the most productive you will ever spend in the kitchen. Relish them.

And a final note: it's always better to turn off the heat when the eggs seem slightly underdone. They will continue to cook in the time between extinguishing of heat and serving onto the waiting plates – which should be heated, by the way, so that the eggs don't cool rapidly when they land there. A piece of toast is all they need to make you happy.

OMELETTE

The slow-and-gentle rule for eggs becomes inoperative if the eggs are destined for transformation into an omelette. Omelette cookery is an exercise in controlled violence. Ingredients: two or three good eggs, beaten well but quickly. A hefty knob of butter. An uncoated frying pan and a large plate, warmed up.

MAYONNAISE

To get the ball rolling, put the pan over a high heat and add the butter. When it's sizzling, swirl it quickly to cover the pan well, then splosh in the eggs. Immediately start tipping the pan so the uncooked egg in the centre of the pan spreads to the edges. When the loose stuff is reduced to a few spoonfuls, and the underside is golden brown, the omelette is ready to turn out. Important: don't be tempted to keep cooking till the omelette is dry all the way through. It will keep cooking even when you've turned it out.

Turning out is sometimes considered the hardest part of omelettery, but it's a cinch. Position the pan just over the plate and start sliding out the disc. When the first half has freed itself from the pan, quickly lift and turn the pan so the top half folds over the plated half. This may take a few attempts to get right. The result? A perfect domestic omelette. You'll get better each time you do it. You will be very happy.

An omelette with a filling is a little more complicated, but it isn't rocket science. Have the filling ingredient(s) at the side of the hob, finely chopped or grated, or in a small frying pan if they have been cooked (such as sliced mushrooms). Don't use too much of them or they may be hard to handle when turning out. When the omelette is nearing the point where it needs turning out, scatter the filling ingredients on the half of the egg-disc that will go onto the plate first. Slide out as described, then turn the naked half onto the filled half. Done.

If you trust your eggs, make mayo while the sun shines. You need: egg yolk, around 100ml of oil, pinch of mustard, a few drops of lemon or vinegar, salt and pepper. You don't need: skill. Hardware of choice? If you've never made mayo before, do it with a hand-held whisk the first time. Just to see how it's done, and to connect with the spirits of your cooking ancestors. After that: blender, electric whisk, or a food processor. They're just too easy to make the hand-held option seriously worth considering, and the results are identical.

OK. Plop the yolk in a clean bowl and add the mustard and acid. Whisk. Add a few drops of oil and whisk till yolk and oil become one. Add a little more oil and repeat. Just carry on this way until the stuff looks like mayonnaise, smooth and silky. At this point you can start adding oil a bit faster.

But please: not too fast. When mayo curdles ('breaks'), it's usually because of impatience. Fortunately, breakages can be mended. Put another yolk (or more mustard) in a new bowl and add the curdled mayo as if it were oil.

Mayonnaising in a machine works faster, naturally, but you still have to add oil carefully. As motor-mayo thickens it makes a telltale 'flub-flub' sound. Translation: OK to add oil a bit faster.

On Bad Mayo days, eggs and oil separate and simply will not go joined-up. The solution? Pass the Hellmann's.

CLARIFIED BUTTER

Fat is forever – and I'm not talking about arterial plaques. Pure fat will keep almost indefinitely in a refrigerated, airtight container. That's one reason to clarify butter, which means removing all traces of water and protein. The culinary reasons: it can be used at higher heats than unclarified butter, and is therefore suitable for roasting and frying; and it is the medium of choice for sealing potted shrimps, pâtés, anything you need to protect from the ravages of oxygen.

Sound good? Then unwrap at least 250g of butter (it is not worth making smaller quantities) and put it in a small saucepan over a low heat. As it melts, it will separate into butterfat, water, protein, and a few other bits. Some of the undesirables will rise to the top; skim them off carefully with a small spoon, doing your level best not to take away any of the butter.

Fully melted? Then choose between east and west. West: pour the butter through a sieve lined with muslin or paper towels, taking great care to leave behind the watery whey residues on the bottom of the pan. This means losing a bit of butter. Tough. East: leave the butter to cook for a while, so the residues brown. Important: use a very, very low heat so the butter doesn't splatter too much as the trapped water boils. When the bubbling has come almost to a complete stop and the solids are a moderately deep mahogany brown, strain through muslin. Browning imparts a nutty tang to the finished product, which is called ghee in Indian cooking. Eastern or western, it's useful stuff.

SHORTCRUST PASTRY

Shortcrust? Easy. Locate a recipe in any reliable cookbook or follow this version: 300g plain flour, 250g butter cut into cubes, a little salt and sugar, 50-100ml ice-cold water. Now make the pastry. Is that all? Naaaah. We're gathered here to address three crucial points. Your recipe says to put the flour in a bowl (or food processor), cut the butter into teensy pieces till the blend resembles coarse breadcrumbs, then add water and blend till you have a ball of solid, workable dough. Fine. Now – the problems.

Problem A: cold. The butter should be very cold so it softens minimally while you're working it. Solution: cut the butter into pieces and then return to the fridge (or freezer) before making the pastry. Problem B: water levels. If you add water till the dough seems wet, you'll end up with a gummy, useless mass. Solution: add water gradually and stop when the mixture seems barely able to form a coherent mass. If a scrap of dough holds its shape when squashed between your fingertips, it's done.

Problem C: cold part 2. Room temperature, body temperature, friction – enemies of nascent pastry. Solution: work fast. Get the finished dough back in a cold climate ASAP. Chill right down before the rolling pin comes out. That's it. Pie-time.

ROUGH PUFF PASTRY

Proper puff pastry? No thanks. I'll perfect it in my next life. But rough puff? Now you're talking. It's faster, easier, and 90 per cent as good. Of the four or five recipes I've used, the fastest to describe is Julia Child's, published in her great book *The Way to Cook*. We can just about cover it if we cut to the chase. To wit: start with c., 500g of ordinary shortcrust pastry (see page 17). Roll it out to make a rectangle around 300mm x 150mm about 6mm thick. Now spread the upper two thirds with a good-size chunk of softened butter, around 30g (1 oz) and fold it: unbuttered section first, then top third down on top of that. Neaten the edges to make them as square and straight as poss., then repeat the roll/butter/folding operation using another ounce of butter. Chill for at least 45 minutes to firm up the butter.

Chilled? Then square out of the fridge. Repeat the rolling and folding, with no butter this time. Neaten edges. Mark the side facing you with a little nick. Refrigerate. Remove from refrigerator. Turn the square so the nick is on the right, and roll and fold one more time. Neaten edges.

Phew! Done. Rough 'n' ready. Refrigerate before use or freeze. It really is about that easy. Just make sure you neaten those edges, refrigerate as prescribed, and roll out to uniform thickness. Thank you, Julia.

RISOTTO

First, the really good news. You know the old rule about stirring risotto constantly while adding hot stock bit by bit? It isn't strictly true. The results will stack up pretty nicely if you go the lazy route, namely: start with two thirds of the stock and give a good long stir to prevent sticking. Let that simmer down till nearly dry, then add the rest of the stock with another good stir. Stir occasionally. It works just fine.

Now the good news: making risotto by the stir-crazy method is neither difficult nor exacting. There are just five tips for perfection. First: if you're beginning by cooking garlic or onion in butter, cook it gently for at least fifteen minutes to soften the harsh allium edges. Second: when the rice goes in, stir it for a good couple of minutes. Third: if you're adding wine before the stock goes in, let it cook down completely. Fourth: use a light stock, so that strong meat flavours will not dominate. And unsalted stock please, because the salt is concentrated as the water evaporates during cooking

Fifth: turn off the heat when the grains retain a chalky crunch at the centre and let it finish cooking on its own. If you keep it over heat till completely done, it will be overcooked when it reaches the plate. Who wants that? Consult your recipe. Concentrate on this quintet of tips. Risotto perfection.

FRYING ONIONS

A renowned cookery writer told me that some publishers put pressure on cookbook writers to lie about frying onions at the beginning of recipes. As in: 'fry the onions till they're soft.' These mendacious publishers, according to my informant, tell writers to say this will take two or three minutes. They fear that readers will switch off if they see that such a mundane preliminary process takes longer. But any attentive cook knows perfectly well that it does.

When you fry onions at the beginning of a dish, you want them to soften more or less completely, become translucent and then (sometimes) take on a little bit of colour without charring, and turn from eye-wateringly, breath-foulingly pungent to mild and sweet. How long does it take? To find out, I sliced four onions, each the size of a satsuma, and put them in a 24cm non-stick pan with 15ml (1 tbsp) of oil over a medium heat – around the heat you would use to fry an egg. I set a timer to go off every two minutes, and I stirred.

Two minutes after the onions had started sizzling, they were hot and somewhat flexible but still tasted raw. After four minutes, most were floppy but still crunchy, the sharp edge of flavour gone but still tasting essentially raw. After six minutes, crunch was turning to chewiness and there was softness in parts; flavour, still pungent. Eight minutes: the onions could be called al dente, and starting to taste cooked. Only at ten minutes were most truly soft, colouring perceptibly, and turning sweet. At around fifteen minutes they were a tangled, slightly gooey, amber-coloured

mess, ready to receive whatever edifice was destined for their sweet foundation. Or just salted, peppered, and served as a condiment.

Of course, there are other ways to fry an onion. If you want to sweat them – soften without colouring – then you have to use the very low heat you'd use for scrambled eggs and figure on a good 20-30 minutes with regular stirring. If you want them to blacken in spots while softening, use a high heat and stir constantly (around 3 minutes in an uncrowded pan). Everything will go faster if you're using a thin, cheap

SAUSAGES

There is more to sausages than meets the eye – and we're not just talking about industrial-grade bangers made from equal parts of hog nostril, flour and water. A curved, tubular object is not easy to cook: you need to use heat wisely and moderately. Wisely in the sense that heat should be applied as uniformly and thoroughly as possible, so that browning is at least modestly consistent. Moderately in the sense of fairly gentle, so the skin doesn't blacken while the interior is still cooking through. A frying pan is not ideal because too little of the tube comes into contact with it, unless the bangers are wading in oil (failure on the wisdom as well as calorie front). A grill can get too hot, and needs constant attention.

In my view, a combination of dry heat and oily heat is best. This means a hot oven – 200C/400F/Gas 6 at least. Put a film of oil in a roasting tin that will hold the bangers with room to spare, and heat it in the oven for 5-10 minutes. Now put in the sausages, and pop the tin straight back in the oven. Turn after 5 minutes, or when the sausages are well browned underneath, and continue to cook till they're done – 10-20 minutes, depending on their girth and the oven's heat. One or two more turns will help.

If bangers in the oven go against your personal grain, a low heat on the grill will do fine. So will the barbecue, if you can keep the bangers from cooking too fast; place them over the coolest part of the coals. But that oven can't be beat. Trust me.

pan – but then you'll end up with a lot of charring.

The mendacity of those publishers, and a detailed examination of a couple of dozen cookbooks, has led me to formulate the Onion Test for determining quality in recipe writing. If a recipe says you can soften onions (without significant colouring) in two or three minutes, treat it with suspicion. If no time is specified, the author is cowardly, lazy, or something worse. If you see the words 'ten minutes' in the first paragraph, you know you're in good hands. Try it yourself, and sue me if I'm wrong.

THE PERFECT...
ONION SOUP

The classic soupe à l'oignon is truly a formidable beast – and you can pronounce that 'formidable' in either French or English with equal precision. A blazing-hot crock of beef stock stuffed with well browned, custard-soft onion shreds, buried under a cap of croutons and molten Gruyère thick enough to stand on. And with calorie-count and fat content large enough to raise a nutritionist's blood pressure to 280 over 190. It's amazing, it's magnificent. But how often would you want to eat it, except on a cold, drizzly January night in Paris? What's needed is a modern version of this trencherman's delight, something suitable for lighter diets and all-weather eating.

I've come across just such a specimen from the kitchens of my indescribably wonderful local gastropub, the Junction Tavern in London NW5. Their version was so delicious that I got them to share it.

The keys to oniony success chez Junction are simple. One: they use a combination of chicken stock and vegetable stock. Two: they add depth of flavour with dry cider, and with extra aromatic ingredients (garlic and herbs) cooked along with the onions in a combination of extra virgin olive oil and butter. Three: they give the onions a really long spell of gentle cooking – something I heartily endorse, as you'll see on page 20 – but without letting them colour. Around 45 minutes should do the trick, with regular stirring. The onions' pungent components (mainly pyruvic acid) and the tear-inducing thiopropanal S-oxide are broken down, leaving the flavour of the natural sugars to develop. But no browning, please.

Their trick is to cook the onions for a relatively short time in the liquid – chicken stock first. This creates a soup in which flavours are harmonious yet distinct: you can sip the cidery broth while getting all that mild onion sweetness as a separate and unique pleasure. The soup is better the next day, and when reheated should be 'loosened up' with vegetable stock. Toast croutons made from baguettes, grate Gruyère or Parmesan or mature Cheddar, and you're away.

Here is the recipe given to me by the Junction Tavern, courtesy of their chef Nick Fraser Stansby. I have made minimal adaptation here, even though Mr Fraser Stansby's method for chicken stock differs radically from my own. His vegetable stock, however, is better than any I had ever made.

Serves 6
5 large white onions
2 cloves garlic
1 large sprig of thyme and rosemary
30ml (2 tbsp) olive oil
25g (1oz) unsalted butter
1 litre (1½ pints) dry cider
1 litre (1½ pints) chicken stock or good-quality chicken stock cubes if necessary
400ml (14fl oz) vegetable stock
Around 150g (6oz) grated Gruyère, Parmesan or mature farmhouse Cheddar
1 baguette for croutons
Sea salt and freshly milled white pepper

Finely slice the onions, and crush the garlic to a paste. Place the onions, garlic, herbs, olive oil and butter into a heavy-bottomed pot, and cook over a very low heat for 40-45 minutes, stirring regularly and taking care not to colour the onions.

Add the cider to the onions, and bring to the boil. Simmer for 10 minutes, then add the chicken stock. Bring to the boil and simmer for a further 10-15 minutes. Season with sea salt and freshly milled white pepper.

This soup is far nicer to eat the next day, so, when reheating, add a ladle or two of the vegetable stock to loosen it.

To serve, cut the bread into 1.25cm (½ in) slices and toast lightly on both sides, place 25g (1 oz) of cheese on top and brown under the grill, pour the soup into a warm bowl and place a crouton on top.

If you intend to make your own stocks here are two short recipes from the Junction.

Chicken Stock: Place the carcass of your left-over roast chicken in a large pan of cold water, along with 75g (3 oz) each of onion, celery, leek and carrot. Add one bay leaf, a sprinkling of fennel seeds and white peppercorns, a sprig of thyme, a clove of garlic and a glass of dry white wine. Bring to the boil and simmer gently for no more than an hour.

For Vegetable Stock: Omit the chicken and double up the quantities of vegetables; cook for 20-25 minutes only. Add a handful of your favourite fresh herbs at the end and steep for five minutes. Strain through a sieve and they are ready to use.

GAZPACHO

Gazpacho is a curiosity. Salad disguised as soup, food that quenches the thirst. One of the few great dishes made without any cooked ingredients. And the only place (apart from a compost heap) where green peppers serve a useful purpose.

Making gazpacho is mostly a matter of sieving and chopping vegetables. It poses just one challenge: not losing patience with that tedious, painstaking work. Last time I made it, I counted the minutes at c., 40 and the tedium factor at c., 1,000.

Think it's worthwhile? Then proceed. To feed six: 1kg of red, ripe, soft tomatoes, attacked in a blender along with a small onion and garlic clove. Frog-march through a fine sieve or squeeze through muslin, and expect to spend a really long, boring time doing it. Chill overnight and rest your arms. The next day, add the same volume of tomato juice, a good splash of vinegar, salt and pepper. Back into the fridge, because it's knife-time. Cut a few skinned, seeded tomatoes into tiny dice. Skin and de-seed one large or two small cucumbers, and cut them into dice of approximately the same size. One medium onion and the miraculous green pepper, minced with a knife; the food processor doesn't give good control over mincing. You are bored, but you are done. Chill everything, covered, until needed.

Show-time: soup into bowls. Dribble of olive oil in each one. Guests and soup to table. Salad in a soup bowl. Urgent dish for late summer. Curious, perhaps. But heavenly.

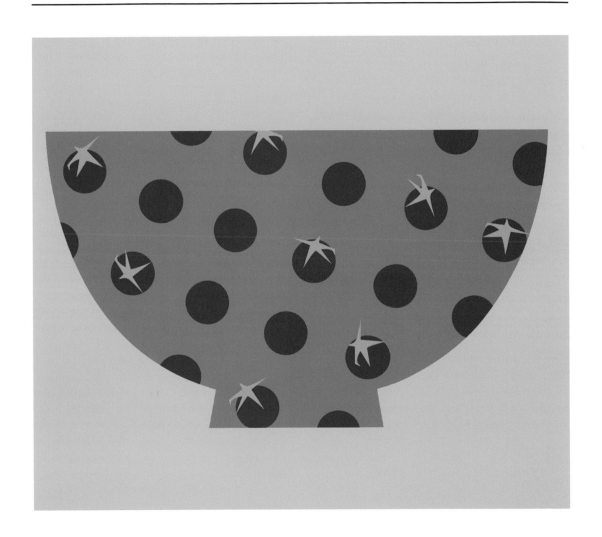

CHEAPO CHICKPEA SOUP

In cold weather, you're crazy not to embrace the Perfect conception of the Perfect cheapo soup. This is a generic term for a whole family of thick liquids, chunky or smooth, that have one thing in common: they all originate in a bag of chickpeas.

Why chickpeas? It isn't just because they're cheap, though they certainly are that. It's also because they have more flavour than many of their competitors – a kind of nutty, creamy richness – and because

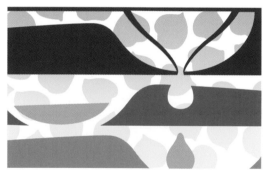

they give up their starch readily. The cheapness is a bonus – but a fairly large bonus, I have to admit. If you buy dried chickpeas, and use them with suitably cheap ancillary flavourings, you can end up spending as much as 30p a head for a range of soupy dishes that will send everyone into a sated swoon.

Before you can make the soup, however, you need to cook the chickpeas. And this is not always a bowl of cherries. Chickpeas (really a seed) may be very elderly, and the older they are, the longer they take to rehy-

drate and cook. I've seen chickpeas that failed to soften significantly even after four hours in the cooking pot. The miracle solution: add a teaspoon or so of bicarbonate of soda to the cooking pot. This cuts simmering time to as little as fifteen minutes, which almost qualifies those seeds for classification as fast food. When they're soft, you're ready to make soup.

My chickpea favourites are puréed soups, leaning heavily on thoroughly softened alliums (shallots, garlic, onion) and flavourings of your choice. Essential point: cook those extras well before you add the precooked chickpeas for final simmering. Our local heroes: cumin, coriander, and/or fennel seeds, cooked with the softened alliums till they release their fragrance. Chickpeas in, water or stock to cover by several inches, simmer for an hour or two. Purée till the blender cries uncle. Thin as needed. Sharpen flavour with salt and pepper, and maybe a little chilli sauce and/or lemon. Chickpea heaven.

The other approach calls for leaving the seeds whole and simmering them with veggies in chunks. The veg should be natives of low cost. Cabbage. Leeks. Carrots. Cauliflower. Plus the essential alliums, which chickpeas just can't live without. Decent stock is a plus here, though a cube will do fine. If you add a tin of tomatoes and a handful of small dried pasta shapes, you'll be imitating pasta e ceci, that southern Italian stalwart. A sprinkling of freshly grated Parmesan might bring the bill per portion up to 38p. Meal in a bowl. Wintertime blues? Banish them with chickpeas.

FISH SOUP

Subject: the velvety soupe de poisson of French cuisine. Stature: classic. Difficulty: low. Three essential words: Garbage, Complexity, Texture. Garbage = heads, bones and trimmings, the only fish you need. If you want whole fish as well, use cheap stuff (especially gurnard). Only requirement: it must be white fish, ideally with some flesh attached and scrupulously trimmed of blood, gills, etc. (See Fish Stock, page 9, for more detail on what needs to be trimmed.) Freezing scraps till you have enough is a good idea. Making friends with the fishmonger is an even better idea – they will usually hand over trimmings for free.

Complexity = lots of supporting flavours to heighten, deepen and lengthen the flavour of the dish. First stop: diced onions lightly coloured in olive oil, followed by garlic and celery cooked for a few minutes more without browning. Second stop: parsley, orange peel, herbs and spices (fennel seeds, thyme, bay leaf, saffron etc.), salt and pepper, tin of tomatoes. Cook briefly, perhaps 10 minutes at a steady simmer, then add the fish. Cover with water. Bring to the boil. Turn down heat to very low. Simmer for an hour at most, and thirty minutes should do it. You test by tasting the fish. If it's essentially flavourless, that means its flavour has passed into the soupy medium. Drain soup through a colander into a clean saucepan. Bin the crud.

Texture = a little thickness and body, easily attained. Toss in a handful of small pasta or finely chopped potato, and boil till the interlopers are soft to the point of dissolution (15-25 minutes). Blend to smoothness, for a lightly creamy texture. Classic garnishes: rouille and grated Gruyère. Acceptable garnish: a dollop of crème fraîche. Result: pleasure.

THE PERFECT...

FISH PASTE

When one needs to assemble lots of nibble-worthy treats for everyone to munch on at odd times of the day, at Christmas for instance, one's thoughts turn naturally to fish paste. Though some will call it fish pâté. I don't want to display too proudly my infinite capacity for pedantic nitpicking, but fish pâté is not the name of what's on the menu here. Namely: a pot or bowl of minced fish flavoured with onion (or shallots), lemon juice, salt and pepper, and tasty lipids (butter or extra virgin olive oil). If you want to get fancy, but not necessarily more accurate, you can call it rillettes de poisson.

The first choice to be made by cut-and-pasters is the fish du jour. As a rule, fattier fish with firm texture is top of the list: mackerel springs to many minds, and so does salmon. Boned, skinned, and lightly cooked. Or smoked, which gives extra flavour for no extra work. But don't use your best smoked salmon for this, please. If you want to do all the addition of fat yourself, try smoked trout, the fish I've been using with great results. Perfect texture, and you can contribute fat in your own chosen amount and form.

Making the stuff couldn't be easier. As a baseline, think about these measurements: 125g of fish, 20g of onion, juice of half a lemon, salt and pepper, and 15ml (1 tbsp) of fattening stuff. This will produce a mildly sharp, fairly dry mix, which can be corrected in any way you like. To this formula I'd be certain to add plenty more lemon and fat, since tang and cohesiveness are major-league desiderata here.

I don't need to say that pasting's best done in a food processor. Nothing gives a clean, uniform result so swiftly and efficiently. Chop the onion first, till it's essentially liquid, then add the rest and fire away. But it can also be done with a knife, a fork, some elbow grease and patience. Chop the onion as fine as poss, then the fish. Put everything in a stout bowl with generously sloping sides, and mash with the back of the fork. Grainier texture than food-processed paste, but no one will hate you.

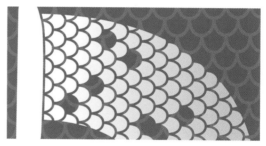

The beauty of these things is that they can be corrected for days after you make them: they should spend at least 24 hours in the fridge before serving, tightly covered with clingfilm. And they will go on being delicious for four or five days. As an ongoing munchable, keep it in the mixing bowl. For a semi-impressive dinner-party starter, pack it into ramekins or unmould it with two teaspoons to form imitation quenelles. For your own satisfaction, vary flavourings at will: spice, lime, vinegar, garlic. You name it. As long as you don't name the results fish pâté.

CHICKEN LIVER PÂTÉ

Every omnivore needs to know how to make chicken liver pâté. It's as easy as falling off a log. It's cheap. It can be made from common ingredients of no great splendour. It freezes dreamily. And it is, of course, fantastically delicious.

The exercise begins with around 450g (1lb) of chicken livers, which may be fresh or frozen. Trim off any yellow/green bits, any stringy bits, and anything that shows the colour of blood. Give them a quick wash, then let them drain in a sieve and finally dry them well. When they're ready, you're ready for action.

Beginning by: gently cooking garlic and shallots (two of each) in lots of butter till they're very lightly coloured. Splash in booze: a short slug of cheap ruby port, Madeira, vermouth, cognac, or just dry white wine. Season with salt, pepper and herbes au choix, and cook till most of the wet stuff evaporates. Remove to a blender. Now melt more butter in the same pan. Add the prepared chicken livers, and cook with frequent stirring till medium-rare (rosy interiors), around 3 minutes. Put them in the blender too, with every iota of residue from the pan.

OK, motor roaring and blend the hell out of the mix. Get it as smooth as possible, but don't even think about putting it through a sieve unless you're extremely patient and extremely strong. (Chefs do this, but they have underlings to do the hard work for them.) If you do feel like torturing yourself, however, use a medium sieve rather than fine. If you can't be

bothered, just scrape the mixture into a serving bowl. When it's warm to the touch, mix in well softened butter – around 20 per cent of the weight of the livers. Taste for salt and pepper. Turn out into a serving dish

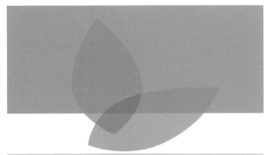

or ramekins. Done. Leave overnight or freeze. Mmm.

Variations? Plentiful. Use cream instead of butter, or (for an airy texture) whipped egg whites. What does not vary: the excellence and ease of this dinner-party stalwart. To know it is to love it.

CHICKEN WITH 40 CLOVES OF GARLIC

If you love chicken and love garlic, but have never eaten chicken with 40 cloves of garlic, you've been leading a deprived life. That's the bad news. The good news: you're in for one of the greatest food experiences of your life. To make it happen, gather a top-quality chicken, four heads of firm, sprightly garlic, some decent (though not bank-busting) extra virgin olive oil, and a big, heavy casserole.

There is some disagreement about the best way to cook this incredibly simple dish, mostly focusing on whether you should (a) use a whole chicken or chicken pieces, (b) peel the garlic or leave the husks on, and (c) brown chicken and/or garlic before the real cooking begins. Point (a): both work fine. Point (b): do not peel under any circumstances (for reasons to be explained below). Point (c): browning chicken is optional; browning garlic is a big mistake in my view, as the aromatic bulbs can get overcooked and bitter-tasting. I should note, however, that other cooks brown first and report that the garlic comes to no harm.

So, my preferred method: preheat the oven to anything in the neighbourhood of 200C/400F/Gas 6. Remove every bit of visible fat from the cavity of the chicken, and brown it or don't brown it, as you see fit; I used to, but don't bother anymore. Separate the heads of garlic and remove loose bits of papery husk, but don't peel the cloves. If you haven't browned the chicken, put it in the pot with a generous film of oil. Turn it to coat with oil.

Now strew the garlic around the chicken, and pour in oil. How much? An absolutely disgraceful quantity. Half a pint (300ml) is not unheard of. The garlic has to stew in the stuff. Toss the cloves in it, and season with salt and pepper, plus some herbal material if you wish. Bring to a modest sizzle on the hob. Cover tightly. Oven, around 50-60 minutes or possibly somewhat less for chicken pieces. Baste a couple of times. Danger point: garlic getting deeply browned but chicken still has a way to go? Remove the garlic with a slotted spoon and put the pot back in the oven. Reunite them before serving.

When the dish is done, you are left with meltingly soft, mildly flavoured garlic cloves which have steamed and stewed inside their husks. Eat them by squeezing the flesh out onto a forkful of chicken, a fragment of toast, or your tongue. This is the best part of the dish, and is one reason that even vegetarians can enjoy chicken with 40 cloves of garlic. Just leave out the chicken, and cook garlic and oil on their own to serve with veg, spuds or rice. (See the item on page 107 for further advice.) Leftover oil? Apply it to salads, veggies, just about anything. This dish is nirvana, reached in around 15 minutes of easy work.

CHICKEN WINGS

A recent survey found that 98 per cent of true chicken-lovers regard the wings as one of the best parts of the bird. I count myself among the 98 per cent, even if an immediate qualification is required. Namely: these can't just be any old wings. The 'value packs' of wings from tasteless industrial birds, sold by supermarkets and low-rent butchers, will not do. You need wings from a proper free-range bird. If your supplier doesn't regularly sell wings in large quantities, grab the odd pair when you find them and freeze till you have enough for a meal. When you're ready,

defrost and consider two winged victories.

Victory the first: comes from braising. Joint them (humerus, radius, wing tip), and use the tips to add collagenic richness to chicken stock. Heat a bit of oil in a heavy frying pan and lightly brown the wings (do this in batches), transferring them to a heavy casserole as they're all done. Now add flavourings, your choice. My favourite, based on a recipe from Craig Claiborne and Virginia Lee's *Chinese Cookbook* (out of print), partners 450g (1 lb) of wings with garlic and ginger (quickly stir-fried in the pan), a 400g tin of tomatoes,

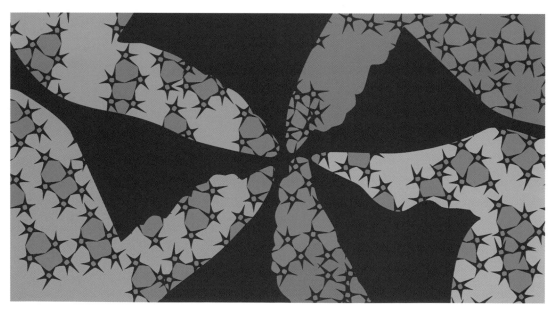

the alliums, 15ml (1 tbsp) each of soy sauce and Worcester sauce, and a generous splash of red wine vinegar. Bring to the boil, then cover and simmer vigorously for 25-35 minutes; toss them once or twice. Important point: don't overcook, as even wings in a watery medium can dry out. Quasi-imperative point: serve with rice.

Victory the second: baked wings. This is simpler in one sense (less preparation, one-step cooking), but more complicated in that you have to keep an eye on them. Essential prelim: coating the jointed wings with oil, around 45ml (3 tbsp) per 450g of wings. This is easiest if you put the wings in a big bowl and toss them in the oil with your hands. If you want to get fancy, season the oil – and you won't regret it, I promise. A herb-and-spice mix comprising ground cumin, coriander, thyme, chilli powder will do just fine. Plus salt and a lot of black pepper. And a splash of wine, water or stock to keep them moist.

Whether plain or fancy, baked wing-things will need 20-25 minutes in a 200C/400F/Gas 6 oven. Baste once or twice. Tricky point: the wings must be in a single layer; use two pans if necessary. Telling point: they're done when the skin feels papery and the muscles in the radius (middle section) feel separate when poked. Refreshing point: if the wings are spicy, serve with cucumber raita or something similar. And final point, in case you were wondering: the source of the survey quoted in the first sentence? I made it up. But everything else here is true.

ROAST DUCK

Mmmm, roast duck. Crisp skin, juicy pink flesh. That's the good news. The bad: perfection isn't easy to achieve on every single outing. First of all, the duck may be Aylesbury, Gressingham, Barbary – nearly anything except Donald. Second, these birds store a lot of subcutaneous fat over very lean flesh, which can overcook while you're melting the fat and aiming for that glorious crunchy skin. A tricky business. This is not helpful advice. But it's true.

In helpful terms, here is my suggestion for big ducks (2.25kg/5 pounds-plus) with their ultra-thick padding of fat. It needs long cooking – and special treatment – so the fat can literally melt out. Easy method with generally reliable results, filched from *The Joy of Cooking*: 3 hours at 120C/250F/Gas ½ (breast down), then turn over and finish briefly at 180C/350F/Gas 4 to crisp the skin. Standard treatment to aid fat-rendering: prick the skin all over, taking obsessive care not to pierce the flesh.

Smaller ducks, such as the delicious Barbary, have less subcutaneous fat. Prick that skin, then deliver a short, sharp cooking shock. Figure on 45-60 minutes at 230C/450F/Gas 8, but watch like a hawk. Just remember: practice makes perfection, most of the time. And even the semi-successes will taste great.

If you have the time and energy, here is an even better-paved road to success with duck.

THREE-PHASE DUCK
The best way to cook a whole duck, in my experience

– and to cook goose as well – is by steaming it, then braising it, and finishing with a blast of roasting to crisp the skin. Seems like a lot of work, and there is unquestionably more than with conventional roasting. But the result is more likely to produce tender flesh, ample rendering of subcutaneous fat, and crisp but not scorched skin than in any other method I have used.

The method comes originally from Julia Child's *The Way to Cook*, one of the all-time great cookbooks, but in repeated outings I have modified her method slightly. The version presented here is an amalgamation of her instructions (paraphrased) and my additions. It works best with large-ish, fatty ducks – weight, around 2.25kg (5 lbs).

Step 1: Steaming

Prepare the bird in the usual way: pull out large gobs of fat from the cavity and yank out any stray bits of feather (which often congregate on or around the wings). And don't forget to cut out the wishbone. This makes it much easier to carve these notoriously difficult birds. You can shove some herbs in the cavity if you wish, or a chunk of lemon. Put the bird with breast down on a roasting rack in a roasting tin, or in a casserole if you have one large enough. Fill the vessel with water to a level that's at least 15mm ('/₂ in) below the underside of the bird; the bird should not touch the water. Now, if you're using a roasting tin, cover the bird with a large piece of aluminium foil, trying to keep head space between bird and foil. (The sheet of foil should be much larger than the tin.) Crimp the edges of the foil around the lip of the tin to get as tight a seal as possible. In my experience, the seal is never perfect; just do your level best. If you're using a casserole, just cover with its lid.

Now put the tin/casserole on the hob over a moderate heat and get the water boiling. If you're using a tin, you may notice spots where too much steam is escaping: tuck in the foil at those spots. You will also need to watch the water level, and top it up to make sure the pan doesn't dry out. Steam for 30 minutes or so, long enough to give the skin a bit of 'cooked' colour and to render out a generous helping of fat. If a lot of steam is escaping (from foil in a tin) despite your best efforts to keep it in, 40 minutes will be better.

Step 2: Braising

Preheat the oven to 190C/375F/Gas 5. Carefully lift the duck, on its rack, out of the pan. Pour out the water, making sure you keep the rendered fat for roasting or sautéing potatoes. Put the duck on its rack back in the pan. Now add the following veg and flavourings to the pan, chopping the veg roughly and the garlic fine:

2 cloves garlic
1-2 carrots, depending on size
2 stalks celery
1 medium onion
Herbs of your choice

Put the pan over a low heat to get things sizzling, then add enough wine, stock or just water to come up to a level that just wets the breast of the bird. The stock created by the initial steaming is a good choice of braising liquid if you don't want to use it for gravy. Re-cover the pan and get the liquid simmering on the hob. Now put the pan in the oven and braise the bird for another 30 minutes or so. It is ready for final cooking when the breast feels firm, with just a little bit of spring.

Step 3: Roasting

Remove the bird from the oven and turn the oven up to 200C/400F/Gas 6. NB: Mrs Child recommends a lower temperature, 325F (around 160C/Gas 3). I find that a higher temperature does a better job of browning the skin without overcooking the breast meat.

Uncover the cooking vessel. Turn the bird over so the breast is facing upwards. Roast until the skin is well browned and feels dry to the touch. This will take something like 20 minutes, but may be a little more or a little less.

Remove from the cooking vessel to a carving platter and put back in the oven with the heat off and door ajar. Make gravy from the remaining juices in the pan.

DUCK BREAST

DUCK LEGS

Crisp-skinned, rosy-pink duck breasts are delicious, and only slightly tricky to cook. Restaurants usually brown them savagely on both sides, then finish cooking in the oven. At home, you can do it more simply and easily on the hob.

The prep: put a thick frying pan over a medium heat – erring on the low side if you want to make life even simpler, if a bit slower – and prick the duck skin all over. The cooking: skin down, gentle sizzle, spooning out the fat to save for frying potatoes. Within 10-20 minutes, depending on heat and on subcutaneous fat levels (which in turn depend on breed and rearing conditions), the breasts will be mahogany brown. Salt, turn, and cook at a slightly higher heat for 5-10 minutes more. They should feel barely springy to the touch. Remove to heated plates and rest for a minute. A&E measure: if they're still too pink when sliced, return slices to the pan for a few seconds.

If you're cooking for a crowd, the restaurant method will be better. Do unto the skin as described above, then brown the flesh briefly. Finish in an oven turned all the way up for 10-15 minutes. If you're doing it this way, the initial cooking should be done well in advance, with the final oven-blast taking place while your eager guests are waiting at the table.

One trick you shouldn't try at home: the duck breasts I ate in the restaurant of a so-called celebrity chef. Skin: inedibly undercooked. Flesh: inedibly overcooked. A miracle! One trick you should try at home: careful treatment of the underrated duck legs.

Duck breasts hog the limelight in restaurants and supermarkets, which is silly. But the silliness has a reward: because most cooks like the breast, you'll sometimes find duck legs being sold separately – and for less money. Is lower cost proof of inferiority? Nope.

In a duck, as in any bird, the legs are somewhat tougher than the breast. This is one reason that the commonest leg-cooking proposal is confit, a long simmering in duck fat originally devised as a means of preservation. Modern-cool cookbooks persist in giving confit recipes, which I think is bonkers. How often do you have a litre or two of duck fat lying around, unless you live in Gascogne?

But other duck procedures are eminently practical, and just as delicious as the swankier breast. A few of my faves follow below, all best suited to smaller Barbary and Gressingham ducks.

First option: pan-cooking. The trick with pan-cooking is to make the skin take most of the heat (as it does in the method for duck breast), but at a slow and steady pace so it doesn't cook too quickly. If it browns too far too soon, it will blacken; bummer. Pan: thick. Heat: nice and low. Timing: with skin down, at least 15 and up to 25-30 minutes. Aim: a good mahogany colour. Before turning: dust with salt and pepper, and with powdered spices if you like. After the turn: cook till it's... well, till it's done. Timings are impossible to dictate with accuracy because so much depends on the type of bird and the length of skin-side cooking, but you'll probably be looking at another 5-10 minutes. You may have to press the drumstick down onto the pan's surface for a minute or two.

The procedure can also be carried out using a combination of hob and oven. Proceed as described until you turn the legs, but instead of cooking them on the hob, pop them in a preheated oven, 180C/350F/Gas 4. Oven-going vessel: frying pan if it's oven-proof, a roasting tin if not. Timings: variable again, but estimate 10-25 minutes. What you lose in time you gain in margin of error, since the heat is lower.

There's a third way to take duck legs for a walk, and that is to braise them. This is worth every step, and there are two different ways to take it.

BRAISED DUCK LEGS

Duck legs present two pairs of questions for the would-be braiser. One: do you (a) aim for browned, crisp skin or (b) accept that the skin will be soft, owing to the moist cooking environment of the braising pot? Two: do you (a) aim to cook the legs à point, just to where they're cooked through but still juicy, or do you (b) let them reach the falling-off-the-bone stage?

Answering A to both these questions requires much more care in cooking. Answering B makes life much easier. I will describe procedures for both options.

Again, the usual duck disclaimer. Large ducks take longer to cook at every stage than small ones, and are also likely to have a much thicker layer of fat under the skin. I think that around 1.5kg-2kg (3$\frac{1}{2}$ or 4$\frac{1}{2}$ lbs) is the best weight, with a minimum of fat and very good flavour.

The Easy Way Out

See notes at the very end for flavouring suggestions. If you don't cook with alcohol, substitute the same amount of stock. Quantities serve four.

> 4 duck legs
> Flavourings of choice
> Around 400-450ml (14-16 fl oz) good stock
> Around 100ml (4 fl oz) alcohol of choice

Put the duck legs, skin side down, in a heavy frying pan over a medium heat; no oil is needed because the duck yields so much, but you might want to score or prick the skin to facilitate the rendering of fat. Note: it is essential not to penetrate the flesh with the knife-tip. Let the skin cook until it's a light-medium-brown colour; this can take anything from around 4-10 minutes.

Lightly salt the flesh side of the legs and turn them. Brown the flesh side just till it takes on a bit of colour (3-5 minutes). Now you need to transfer the legs to a casserole if (a) your frying pan doesn't have a lid or (b) you're planning to cook the legs in the oven and your frying pan can't go in the oven. If you're cooking in the oven, turn it on to

180C/350F/Gas 4. Add the flavourings, letting them cook a little in the hot duck fat if you wish, then add the liquids. The aim with the liquids is to come around three quarters of the way up the sides of the duck legs; use less or more as needed.

Bring liquids to a boil, cover the vessel, and cook the duck till it's as buttery-soft as you want: figure on 1½-2 hours in the oven, probably a little less on the hob. Check the liquid level regularly to make sure the pan isn't getting too dry, and top up if necessary; this is especially critical if cooking on the hob. Before serving, carefully degrease the cooking liquid to remove as much fat as possible. The fat is worth saving for cooking vegetables or pulses. Also: taste the cooking liquid before serving. If you want it to be more concentrated, remove the legs to a platter and boil the liquid down hard before serving.

The Hard Way Out
(and much the better way, in my view)
If you want the duck cooked à point, you have to watch your cooking time like a hawk. If you want to have crisp duck skin, you have to brown the legs when braising is finished. The key to successful browning is not to let the skin get too wet in the first place.

> 4 duck legs
> Flavourings of choice
> Good stock and alcohol of choice (for quantities see below)

Put the duck legs, skin side down, in a heavy frying pan over a medium heat; no oil is needed because the duck yields so much, but you might want to score or prick the skin to facilitate the rendering of subcutaneous fat. Note: If you're scoring or pricking, it is essential not to penetrate the flesh with the knife-tip. Let the skin cook until it's a light-medium-brown colour; this can take anything from around 4-10 minutes.

Salt the flesh side of the legs and turn them. Brown the flesh side just till it takes on a bit of colour (3-5 minutes). Now you need to transfer the legs to a casserole if your frying pan doesn't have a lid, or if your pan isn't big enough to hold all the legs in a single layer.

CRUCIAL point: the duck legs must be in a single layer or this method will not work.

HIGHLY ADVISABLE point: this works better on the hob than in the oven, because the hob makes it much easier to control the heat and keep tabs on the cooking.

Add the flavourings, letting them cook a little in the hot duck fat if you wish, then add the liquids. But in this case, the liquids aren't measured by volume. They're measured exclusively by the amount of coverage they give those legs. The aim here is not to cook the skin in liquid at all, so you have to pour in liquid to a very shallow depth, just below skin-level. You can top it up if you need to, but the cooking time is so short that you probably won't.

OK. Bring the liquids to a boil, then turn the heat down to a moderate simmer and cover the pan. Set the timer for 15 minutes and check cooking at that point; the legs are highly unlikely to be done, but you'll get a good sense of how much more time they need. Best testing method by far: prod the thickest part of the thigh with your thumb. Set the timer for 5 minutes and test again; keep repeating this till you think you're just about there. For Barbary duck legs, the usual cooking time is around twenty minutes.

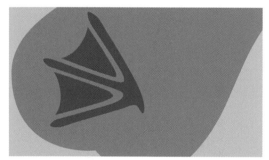

When the legs are just about cooked, preheat the grill to its highest setting; this is where you will brown the skin. Remove the cooked legs from the pan and put them, skin side up, on a rack in your grill pan. Put them under the grill and blast away till the skin is bubbling and crisp (4-10 minutes). In the meantime, reduce the braising liquid if necessary and degrease it thoroughly. When spooning out the braising liquid, make sure you pour it around the duck and not on top, as it would soften up the crisped skin. Note: you can also crisp up the skin with a blowtorch, if you have one in the kitchen for making crème brûlée (see page 117).

FLAVOURINGS FOR DUCK

Few birds, if any, embrace such a diversity of flavourings as enthusiastically as duck. It likes spice, it likes sweet, it likes sour. It positively loves fruit, whether fresh or dried. If your time and energy are limited, flavouring for the recipes here can consist of nothing more than a quick addition of one or two items to the browned duck. e.g.:

- A chopped onion or pair of garlic cloves with a small handful of chopped olives
- A sprinkling of herbs or spices with a spoonful of apricot jam or orange marmalade
- A sliced orange and a little bit of chopped chilli

If you want to get more complicated, aim for a combination of sweetness and pungency.

The only thing you REALLY need to remember when deciding on flavourings: Quick-braising (The Hard Way Out) will not give some ingredients enough time to cook properly. Onions, garlic and dried fruit all fall in this category. Just take these factors into account, so you can pre-cook onions/garlic, for instance, and soften dried fruit in boiled water. There's no end to what you can do with duck legs, the cheapest part of the bird – apart from the quack.

POT-ROASTED PHEASANT

Pot-roasted pheasant (PRP) is greatly superior to 99.9 per cent of the roasted pheasant you are likely to come across. That's because pheasant is a dry bird. Lean as anything, and a quick cooker. If you open-roast it, you're inviting overcooked disaster. The idea that 'draping bacon over the bird keeps the flesh moist'? Hogwash. How can bacon fat work its way through the skin?

So here we go, into a heavy, lidded pot that holds the bird(s) comfortably. Company: flavoursome fluid (including wine, ideally) to moisten the pot generously, and oil or fat to prevent sticking. Seasonings: your pick, but try to include bacon and garlic. Preheated oven, modest temperature (say 180C/350F/Gas 4). Watch the cooking; top up fluid if necessary; start testing after 30 minutes. When the breast is firm to the touch, your PRP is AOK.

There's an even better method for cooking pheasant. And I call it a method rather than a recipe because I want this to be guidance, with you providing the seasonings.

PHEASANT IN TWO PARTS

Start work a good few hours before you plan to serve. You can even do it all the day before, apart from final cooking.

This dish calls for cooking the breast and legs separately, and begins with boning: cutting off the legs and then the breasts. A few tips on this. One: cut out the wishbone before removing the breasts. Two: use a very sharp boning knife or stout-bladed knife of around 8in length. Three: remove the 'oyster' with the legs. Four: take care when working out the breast, because it is (as in all birds) fairly fragile stuff. Five: get the butcher to do this if he or she is willing.

OK. You now have 2 legs, 2 breasts and 1 carcass per bird. Make a stock with the carcass(es), either plain or well furnished with aromatic ingredients such as garlic, onion, celery and herbs.

THE LEGS

These are cooked slowly in a casserole with plenty of liquid and seasonings (which you have to choose for yourself). You can brown the legs first but be warned: they don't brown evenly because of their shape. Put them in the casserole with seasonings of choice. Add liquid (stock, table wine, port or cider) to cover by around 75 per cent. Get the pot simmering on the hob, then cover and finish cooking there or (better) in a coolish oven (c., 150C/300F/Gas 2). It will probably need around 90 minutes of cooking, but timings can vary so check in occasionally. If there's more than one layer of legs, rotate so that those on the top go down to the bottom and vice versa. Add some vegetables for the final 30-40 minutes if you wish.

Once cooked, the legs can be left with the lid ajar and reheated gently just before serving. Desirable item before serving: remove the legs from the pot and cook down the braising liquid to concentrate it. The legs can be returned to the pot for final reheating.

THE BREASTS

Having boned them out, you now see that pheasant breasts are pretty insubstantial things – sometimes barely an inch thick at the thickest point. No wonder they so easily get overcooked in roasting. The way to deal with this is to treat them like a steak and fry them quickly. Heavy pan over medium-high heat. The timings can't be laid down as law because of the usual variables, but I'll be surprised if it takes more than 5-6 minutes.

Lightly salt the skin side and fry that one first, making sure it gets browned. Then salt the flesh side and finish cooking, but please bear in mind that the cooking time is probably going to be shorter for flesh-side than skin-side. Watch the cooking carefully, and test with your trusty thumb or index finger. If the flesh feels soft, it needs more cooking. If it feels hard, it is probably overcooked. Aim for something in between: the flesh should 'give' when pressed, but it should spring back immediately.

Serving

Give each eater one breast and one leg, then spoon some of the cooking liquid from the casserole onto both pieces.

Seasoning Suggestions

Entirely up to you, and it's easy: almost anything tastes good with pheasant. I personally would not braise the legs without garlic, bacon and either European herbs or Middle Eastern spices. Alcohol of choice: ruby port, which goes well with game, and some red wine vinegar added near the end of cooking lends a little sharpness.

QUICK PHEASANT

Pheasant is usually roasted or pot-roasted, but here's an idea for cooks in a hurry: if you halve the bird, you can cook it quickly in a covered frying pan. Ask your butcher to do the division if you wish. For DIY-ers, two vital points: take care not to damage the breast meat, and cut off the backbone so the halves lie flat in the pan.

Ready? Then heat some oil in a thick, heavy frying pan with a lid. Put in the bird halves with skin side down, and cook for a few minutes just to get a little colour. Now turn them over and prepare for the fun part. Namely: adding flavour, anything that you normally combine with a game bird. For me, that means alliums, any variety of cured pork, and whatever wine/stock, herbs and spices happen to be lying around. Liquid: around half an inch deep.

Boil up, lid on, and bubble energetically for around 20 minutes. Test by poking the thickest part of the breast with your thumb. When it shows real resistance, you're there.

THE PERFECT...
PARTRIDGE

Partridge is the user-friendliest of Britain's game birds. At around 300g (10oz), a single bird will feed most diners well. The bones are easily dealt with. Breast and leg cook at around the same clip, so there's minimal danger of uneven timing. And the flavour is excellent, notable less 'gamey' than many of partridge's colleagues in the field of feathered game, but full and rich. Kind of like a guinea fowl with the courage of its convictions. And the cooking? Couldn't be simpler, as long as you remember two things.

One: with a bird this small, you are looking at a short cooking time. Unless you're a member of the old-fashioned school of game cookery, which believes in overcooking the bird murderously and then disguising its Saharan texture with gravy. If you are not of that school, please think of partridge as a 20-something bird. It needs 20-something minutes of cooking, and you're courting disaster if you go much over that. If that sounds like bad news, bear in mind that it makes partridge a prime possibility for midweek dinners.

How to give the birdies their 20-something minutes of fame? By starting them off in a frying pan, which is where the second necessary item comes in. If you want to get colour into the skin, quick browning is the best way to do it. Dry the trussed birds all over, tie the legs together at the drumstick ends if they haven't been trussed, and season with a little salt. Into hot oil. Don't crowd the pan. Turn the birds to brown reasonably evenly all over, especially the breasts. This should take 3-5 minutes in all, and remember: the browning is part of the 20-something formula.

The rest of the time? There's the oven, natch: 15 minutes at a fierce temperature should do the job. But I like wet stuff with partridge, so I think a quick braise is better. A braise with a difference, however. Because the bird will be in the pot such a short time, you need to cook your braising liquid in advance. Brown onions, garlic, bacon etc. in a heavy casserole; season ad lib, adding flour if you want thickness; pour in wholesome liquids (stock and lots of wine). Simmer smartly, to reduce the liquid to the point where a sip makes you think: 'Mmm, good gravy.' Hint: it will probably happen when the fluids have reduced to c., 25 per cent of their original volume. Suggestion: do it in advance. Fancy suggestion: braise cabbage in the casserole instead of gravy, and finish the partridges on top of the greenery.

Ready to braise? Get liquid/cabbage simmering on hob. Put in the browned birds, lying on their sides. Turn after five minutes. Start testing after another five. Remember the 20-something rule. Serve them forth. Partridge family happiness, for 20-somethings (and over).

QUAIL

Funny things, quails. They look too small and gimmicky to be serious birds, and cost too much – around £5 for a packet of 4, which will just about serve 2 – to be an everyday substitute for chicken. Strictly restaurant territory? Nope. Quails really taste good, in a mildly gamey sort of way, even though they're farmed. And they're not difficult to cook even in large numbers, which makes them good candidates for a dinner party.

After a concerted burst of quail-mania, I came to think of these diminutive birds as winged drumsticks. They weigh around the same, and behave the same, as the drumstick from an average-size chicken. That means that you can use them in many of the same ways.

Whatever else you do with quails, don't ignore the cardinal rule: watch out for overcooking. Yeah, yeah, I know: this rule applies with all foods. With quail, however, the imperative looms even larger because there's this tendency to think along the lines of 'whole bird = long cooking.' Not with quail. The target timing, here as with a drumstick, is somewhere in the 15-20 minute range using a fairly high heat. Watch the clock as soon as it strikes 15 minutes, and don't walk away for too long.

The second rule for quail is delicate handling. These little fellows have very thin skin, which is easily torn even by brief contact with a wooden spoon. If you can manage it, handle them by the end of the drumsticks – and with your fingertips, if the heat doesn't make you scream.

With those general principles in mind, you can consider the main options. All call for a brisk heat, though this is least vital with pan-braising. If you're choosing this excellent method, one good tip: cook all the ancillary ingredients first before the bird gets browned and braised. Stir-fry them briskly till they're edible, then remove to a plate and wipe out the pan. Brown the quails quickly, add back the flavourings, put in tasty fluid to keep things wet and provide a gravy. Quails on their sides, turned once; 15-20 minutes or so; eat.

If you're using the oven, remember one thing: even a high heat (230C/450F/Gas 8) will barely brown the skin during such brief cooking. To induce colour artificially, make a glaze of oil and something sugary (honey is ideal) and brush the little birdies with it before they go in. Breasts pointing up, baste once or twice, 15-20 minutes.

Final option: the grill, either indoor or outdoor, particularly good in hot weather. A glaze is useful once again, and use it for basting as well as initial brushing. Moderate-to-high heat, with careful turning to fire up the whole bird. Diminutive birds, substantial pleasure. Eat them with your fingers.

THE PERFECT...

STEAK FOR A CROWD

A ROAST FOR TWO

Steak is an easy dish for a dinner party, but standard cooking methods are impractical if you're cooking lots of them. Restaurant cooking has the answer to the problem, a two-step cooking process beginning with a quick sear. Heat a heavy pan or grill-pan till it's scorching-hot. Turn on the extractor fan. Oil the pan lightly and slap in as many steaks as will fit without crowding. Brown on both sides – this happens pretty fast, just a minute or so – and remove to a platter till all the steaks are done. They can sit till cool if this suits your schedule, and there's a lot to be said for searing well in advance: the kitchen has time to clear of smoke, which is produced in vast quantities by that high-heat browning.

When you're ready for blast-off, preheat the oven to 200C/400F/Gas 6. Put the steaks on flat roasting racks – this is important – in one or two large roasting tins. You need to have the steaks on racks or the undersides will finish cooking in their juices and will go soggy underneath.

Seasoning? Just salt and pepper. Oven hot? Slide the roasting tins onto a rack or racks near the top of the oven. If you're using 2 shelves, move the lower pan to the upper shelf, and vice versa, at some point. Timings? Gotta leave that to you, because there are so many variables, but 10 minutes should do it. And I've never needed more than 15 minutes except for really, really thick steaks. Leave to rest for 5 minutes or so before serving. Sauce if you wish. Your dinner-party friend.

Experts constantly tell us that the nation's favourite food is some exotic import or other. Oh yeah? When I ask someone what meal they would have if they could have anything on earth, they usually answer: 'A Sunday roast.' Only problem: that nostalgic, comfort-me-with-gravy appeal harkens back to the days when families were big and time plentiful. Nowadays many of us live in a household of two, three or even one. How can a twosome wax retro and eat a Sunday roast without massive expenditure of time? Answer: by buying a small joint and proceeding as follows.

Weight matters little here: the ruler rules. Your hunk of meat should be no more than around 13cm at its thickest. Ideal candidates: rolled shoulder of pork, rolled sirloin, chump end of leg of lamb. Crucial point: the joint must be at or close to room temperature. Remove it from the fridge at least three hours before cooking.

Ready? Then heat some oil medium-low in a large, heavy frying pan and brown the meat slowly on all sides. You want to brown it really well, giving it the colour that it won't have time to acquire in the oven. This can easily take twenty minutes, and you should preheat the oven to 200C/400F/Gas 6 in the meantime. NB: take care if you're using pork with the rind on. Full development of crackling will happen in the oven. Brown the rind till it's just colouring and showing first signs of the characteristic bubbles.

While the meat is browning, quarter some spuds

(around the size of a small orange) and par-cook them in boiling water or (better still) the microwave. They should just start to show signs of softness. If you prefer parsnips, do the same with them.

Meat brown, veg par-cooked; the oven awaits. If your frying pan can tolerate the oven, just put the spuds/snips around the meat, spoon oil over them, and slide the pan into the oven. If pan and oven don't mix, transfer the meat to a roasting tin and put the veg around it. Pour frying oil over veg. Salt and pepper. Into the oven.

Timing? Variable, but I've never seen this take less than twenty minutes or more than thirty-five. Ample time to cook some green veg. Once out of the oven, the meat should rest for 5-10 minutes while you make a simple gravy. If the spuds need a little more time, remove the meat and let them have it. And when you carve, don't worry if your symbol of nuclear-familial bliss is underdone at the centre. Carve from the ends. There will probably be a bit too much meat for two people, and underdone meat can be recooked the following day by sautéing, brief stewing, or turning into a sauce for pasta. Destination: the good old days. Travelling time: around one hour.

SPANISH TORTILLA

Spanish tortilla, one of the all-time great lunch dishes: easy, cheap, and equally delicious served hot, warm, or room temperature. To make it a master-piece, remember two vital points and two tricks. First vital: don't think of tortilla as eggs with a potato and onion filling but as potato and onion bound with eggs. For each egg provide a big spud, and onion to taste – anything from a slice to a whole (smallish) onion per egg. Second vital: don't stint on olive oil for frying. Sufficient: a depth of around 3mm ($\frac{1}{8}$ in) in a heavy, preferably non-stick frying pan.

First trick: cook the potatoes in water; the stan-dard frying MO more than doubles cooking time, and adds calories and mess. Simmer the potatoes instead (peeled and sliced 3mm/ $\frac{1}{8}$ in thick) till barely soft enough to eat. Takes ten minutes or so.

In the meantime, and it will be around the same time it takes to cook the spuds, cook the onions in a good glug of extra virgin olive oil (around 45ml /3 tbsp) in your frying pan. You are aiming to colour them lightly and soften them considerably. When the spuds are done, drain them. When the onions are nice and limp, put in the spuds and mix in well. Pour in the eggs. Let the whole mess cook at a gentle heat. Don't fiddle with it. It needs no help.

Trick two: don't try to turn the tortilla; this is a royal pain in the butt. When there's just a shallow puddle of wet egg on top (after 5-10 minutes) and the bottom is crusty-brown, finish the cooking under the grill. Grill-time: 2-3 minutes, just long enough to

set the tortilla and brown it lightly. Now run a thin, flexible spatula under the whole underside of the tor-tilla to make it separate easily from the frying pan. Put a large plate over the pan and, holding it firmly in place, turn the pan over so the tortilla settles neatly on the plate.

Serve straight from the pan or at anything warmer than room temperature. Easy. Delicious. And infinitely malleable: there's almost nothing you can't add to a tortilla.

30-MINUTE CHICKEN DINNER

This quick chicken dinner has been one of the most popular quick fixes among readers and friends with whom I have shared it. To make the dish, you need chicken pieces – leg or breast, though legs, of course, were first in line when God was handing out flavour. They must be from a good chicken. You need some wine, or sherry, or vermouth. An onion and/or some garlic. A few seasonings.

Oven: 200C/400F/Gas 6 – or higher if you're in a real hurry. Chicken: into a roasting tin, with sliced onions/garlic around it or underneath. Bacon in the fridge? Put a rasher of two of that in, too. Now pour in enough wine to create a pool of liquid around 5mm (¼ in) deep – and if you don't cook with alcohol you can use stock or water. Season the pool with whatever herbs or spices happen to be around, making sure they get wet and stay wet: if they get prolonged exposure to dry, high oven heat, they may burn. Salt and pepper. Tin into oven. Roast for 35-40 minutes, basting 2-3 times. In the meantime, boil spuds or rice and make a salad. Your pool of flavoured wine becomes instant gravy.

The choice of seasonings is as big as your spice-and-herb cupboard. I cook this at least once a week and my audience never complains that 'we had this the other day.' If you're worried about it, you can instantly transform the dish by squeezing on some lime or lemon juice, or sprinkling each serving with a few drops of superior vinegar.

Different seasonings = new dish. Final result = gustatory Einstein.

SLOTHFUL CHICKEN DINNER

This is a variation on the 30-Minute Chicken Dinner. Buy chicken pieces of the best quality you have access to. Buy carrots, too, and new potatoes whose size is (approximately) that of a walnut. Back at the ranch, preheat the oven to 220C/425F/Gas 7. Peel the carrots and cut into chunks the size (approximately) of the spuds.

Now comes the hard part. Put the chicken pieces in a roasting pan. Throw in whatever seasonings you happen to have. Make sure the seasonings are in the bottom of the roasting pan. Then add the carrots and potatoes.

Still on your feet? Then a wine-glass's worth of water or (better) wine, to keep the pan juices from burning; do make sure the seasonings are wet. Pan into oven; set timer for 10 minutes. At the beep-beep-beep-beep, take the pan out and baste the contents; you may also dust the pan juices with a sprinkling of flour, to thicken the ensuing gravy.

More hard work: put pan back in oven. Timer set for 10 minutes again. Baste when it beeps. Back into the oven, ten minutes more. Everything should be done. If one component isn't, remove whatever is fully cooked and let the remainder have what it needs. Cooking for the slothful.

AFTER-WORK FISH STEW

A proper fish stew takes hours to get on the table. Well, maybe 90 minutes if you know what you're doing – but it's not the sort of thing you would think about rustling up for a midweek dinner. Under pressure from the junior Ehrlichs for ever-more-enticing meals to alleviate the character-building despair induced by AS-levels, GCSEs, and SATs, I devised a procedure that stands that thinking on its head. It requires potatoes, vegetables, and white fish off the bone. And it takes something like thirty minutes from first chop to final ladling.

First chop: when you get home, cut the potatoes

the second choice, stock (which can be meat or chicken, by the way) is numero uno. Put in enough to come around halfway up the depth of the spuds. Cover and bring to a merry boil, then go and cut the veg into chunks of tasteful size; carrots, broccoli, cauliflower and fennel all work well. You may add them to the pot immediately (if you like vegetables to be unfashionably soft) or leave till later. At the same time, cut the fish into chunks and put them where the cat can't reach.

Now go to the fridge, open a bottle of white wine, and pour a small glassful into the increasingly fragrant pot. Cover the pot. Pour an even bigger glass of wine for yourself, and check the pot to make sure it's bubbling merrily. If all's well, go away. Put your feet up. Check your email, deleting ads for cheap mortgages and Viagra. Caress the cat. Tell the children to stop watching TV and do their homework.

In twenty minutes or so, you will return to a kitchen that's smelling great. The potatoes should be just about cooked. If you didn't put the veg in before, add them now and cook, covered, for another five minutes. When you feel certain that you will be ready to eat in another five minutes, put in the fish (single layer, lying on top) and slap the lid on. Call everyone to the table. By the time they straggle in (another five minutes), the fish should be ready for ladling. You will have drunk one more glass of wine, and will be hungry. Life will be good, or a reasonable facsimile thereof.

into uniform chunks of relatively small size – something like 2cm ($^3/_4$ in) will do. Put them in a heavy frying pan or saucepan with some oil or butter, and turn the heat on. While they're preparing to sizzle, cut up the inevitable alliums: garlic and onions both sit happily in this setting. Add to the pan and stir in.

Now add some seasonings. My second favourite: whatever happens to be within arm's reach. Absolute favourite: whatever my hand first encounters at the front of the spice cupboard. Add your random selection to the pot, stir in, and add some liquid: water is

FAJITAS

I am indebted to Ms Rachel Jones of London NW5 for suggesting, while we were waiting to be served at the butchers, the excellence of fajitas for informal, child-friendly meat. Fajitas are a fashionable item, under their own (Mexican) name or the English translation of 'wrap.' I like fajita better. 'Wrap' makes me think of something made from lambs' wool and bundled around the shoulders in cold weather.

A fajita is a soft tortilla, served warm, wrapped around anything small and tasty. Rachel spoke warmly of them because they're a good way of getting children to eat unfamiliar foods. When you serve young children a plate of A, B and C, you are saying: 'This is dinner, take it or leave it.' Cue grumbles and refusals. When you serve those supple discs of griddled dough with a selection of diverse goodies, you are saying: 'Here are the ingredients. Make dinner just the way you want it to be.' What you're doing, to use yet another modish word, is empowering them.

So, to empower: buy ready-made tortillas from any supermarket. Fill bowls with sliced cukes, peppers, tomatoes; shreds of cooked chicken; cooked veg; yoghurt, cottage cheese, grated Cheddar; condiments ad lib; and whatever etceteras happen to be lying around. Heat tortillas. Put everything on the table. Let the young ones make an unholy mess. More empowerment to their elbows.

GRILLED FISH

FRIED SALMON

My approach to grilling fish calls for a departure from the conventional method. Conventional meaning: grill pan, wire rack or grid, turning halfway through cooking. With fish, that's not the best way. This is delicate material, in both flesh and skin. To keep those tissues intact, and the precious internal juices as well, you're better off proceeding with a no-turn method that also has the great advantage of simplifying the cooking process.

Starting by: preheat the grill to its highest setting, with the shelf at a level where the fish will be around 5cm (2 in) from the heat source. Now take out a stout baking sheet or roasting tin and remove the fish from the fridge. If it's a fillet with the skin on, brush the skin with plain oil and place (oiled side down) on the sheet. Brush the top with oil and salt lightly. Anything else, just brush one side and place on the sheet with oiled side down. Brush again with oil or (better) place a good nub of butter on top. Whack under the grill.

Now keep your hands off! Don't turn, lift, or stab. The fish will cook on both sides because of the heat of the sheet. How long? My experiments – salmon fillets, Dover sole, whole red mullet – have all needed around five minutes. Filleted flat fish needs somewhat less time, though not much less. Just keep your eyes, ears and nose open. It's easy to grill fish, equally easy to ruin it by overcooking. Done? Get a metal spatula right under each piece and carefully lift out. Serve with a lemon wedge. Time to eat.

If you have a fillet of good Scottish salmon – and especially wild salmon – one of the best ways to approach it is to fry it slowly in a heavy pan.

Three caveats here. One: the technique works only with fillets rather than steaks, because it's designed to produce delectably crunchy skin – and to simplify cooking by applying the heat mostly to the

skin. Two: you'll get best results by using fillets (unskinned, obviously) that have not been scaled, because the scales provide a protective layer for the skin while contributing considerably to the crunchy appeal. If crunchy skin appeals in the first place, that is. Three: you need to go slowly, since a high heat will blacken the skin before the flesh has cooked adequately.

All three points: no big deal. Numbers one and

two are handled by friendly interaction with the fish-monger. Number three is handled by a laid-back interaction between you, your frying pan and your hob.

OK? Then heat the pan over a low heat with enough oil or fat – duck or goose fat work a treat, vegetable oil will do fine – just to film the surface. Now slide in the fillets, skin side down, and leave them. I mean really leave them. The oil or fat should barely sizzle around the margins of the fillet. The skin takes the worst of the heat, which is slowly conducted through the flesh to cook it slowly and gently.

To tell when you're ready to flip the fillet, look for two things. First: the skin side must be well and truly brown – anything less and it will not be crunchy. Second: the flesh should have lost its raw colour up to around three quarters of its depth from the skin. With a fillet of normal thickness – i.e., any part of the fish except the tail – this should take 12 or 15 minutes. Middle-cut salmon – smack-dab midway between tail and head – is ideal.

When the skin is properly browned, you may find that the flesh is cooked enough for eaters who don't mind eating their salmon with a goodly element of rawness. I fit in that category. If you don't – if you're squeamish in that way – flip the fillets and cook for one or two minutes. Don't let it linger too long: remember, most of the cooking happened while the skin was in contact with the pan. And for serving, do as little as possible: a little lemon or lime is all you need for this seasonal (what's that?) treat.

ROAST SALMON

A whole baked salmon, resplendent in its shimmering skin, is one of the loveliest things you can place on a dining table. It's also a pain in the butt. Often overcooked, unless you're really good at it. A time-consuming mess to skin, cut up and serve. Thanks, but no thanks.

My preferred alternative may look less impressive, but it takes the sweat out of salmon for a crowd. Source: the estimable Clare Macdonald. Her source: John Tovey of the famed Miller Howe restaurant. So much for originality.

The drill is dead-easy. First of all, try to get middle-cut salmon, which should have just the right thickness, but thinner pieces are acceptable. Have the fish filleted but neither skinned nor scaled, and cut it into serving-size portions; these can be anything from 90-180g (3-6oz), depending on the appetites of the audience. Lightly oil a non-stick baking sheet (or sheets) to accommodate all the pieces comfortably; put fish on metal, skin side down; refrigerate (covered) if you're sensibly working in advance.

Show-time: preheat oven to 200C/400F/Gas 6. Drop a dainty chunk of butter on each piece of fish. Now, top of the oven please. Timing: target is 5 minutes, going up to maybe 7-8 if you don't like salmon pink at the centre. The thinner pieces will be well done (for those who like it that way). The skin should have formed a nice crisp crust (ditto). So easy, so quick. Why work hard when all you want to do is sit down and eat?

CURED SALMON

Gravlax achieved gastronomic mega-cool status some time in the 1980s – and became passé in the 1990s, when sushi and tartare took over in the raw-fish trendiness stakes. The Scandinavian version, a.k.a gravadlax, should never have fallen from fashion. It takes neither time nor skill to prepare, and it's delicious. Can we please get it back on the table, perhaps in a revised method that may suit many people's taste better than the original? Ingredients: decent-quality salmon fillets (middle cut is best) with the skin on, fine salt, caster sugar (optional), freshly ground black pepper, and fresh dill.

Most recipes for gravlax assume that you're making it as a party dish. They also prescribe a massive quantity of salt, as much as 500g/18 oz for a whole salmon. Makes sense, because gravlax was originally a preserving method. But since preservation is no longer the principal aim, and no one gives dinner parties anymore, two happy announcements: you can use gravlax as an everyday dish, with smallish quantities, and you can get away with very small quantities of salt. But don't depart from another venerable stricture: removing the small 'pin' bones using tweezers, pliers, or your fingers.

PRESERVED FISH

OK, let's measure salt. Not by weight of fish but by surface area to be covered: for a light cure, with a result that barely tastes of salt, use 2.5ml/½ tsp per 100 sq cm (15 square inches) of salmon; for a heavy cure, you can double or treble that. Measuring pepper, easy: simply grind an even coating over the flesh. Fine pepper gives a milder taste than the traditional coarse grind. Ditto for dill: sprinkle the finely chopped herb evenly, or lay on whole sprigs for a milder taste (and remove before slicing). If you want sugar, which I think redundant, apply in the same way as the salt, and at the same time.

Traditionalists would now tell you to wrap the salmon in foil, put a flat board on top, and weight the board down with something heavy. This is useful for the old-fashioned method – it helps squeeze out water extracted by the salt and sugar – but optional with a light cure. Non-optional: refrigerate the wrapped fillets. Absolute minimum, 36 hours; 48 is better; 72 will be fine, especially if the salt has been generously applied. NB: enthusiastic salination will require the occasional draining of extracted water.

All done. Slice. Serve with the traditional mustard sauce or just with lemon.

The best thing about this method is that you don't have to use it to make gravlax. Plain old salt and pepper will do. Other seasonings are also good: ground spices, different herbs, citrus zest. It's the basic method that counts, as in all cooking. And this method is tops, even if it's no longer cool.

Pickled fish? Surely that's only for people who can their own vegetables and knit their own jumpers. You might think so, but you would be wrong. It's the easiest thing in the world, and almost as satisfying as baking bread. First essential: the freshest fish you can lay hands on, preferably herring or mackerel, filleted by the fishmonger. Second essential: a thorough scrape-and-polish at home, to remove every single trace of blood. Third essential: a sealable vessel that will accommodate the fish in a flat layer or layers.

What's next? Put cleaned fish in vessel and add a 4:1 mixture of water and wine vinegar; you need enough liquid barely to cover the fish. Add a good sprinkling of salt, making sure it ends up in liquid and not on top of the fish. Make sure the brine makes contact with every bit of fish, then cover vessel and refrigerate. Turn the fish when you remember to. It should be edible after two days, though it will survive (and strengthen in flavour) for a couple of weeks.

Of course, this is only half the story. The other half is told by flavourings. Arguable essentials: peppercorns, onions and garlic. Scrumptious peripherals: coriander, bay leaf, dill or celery seeds. Whatever you put in, the story is easily told. And even more easily eaten.

STEWED SQUID

For the purposes of this exercise, squid shall embrace octopus and cuttlefish. (And the earth won't move for any of them.) Why? Because sometimes, though probably not at the supermarket, you get really big squid which you can't fry or stir-fry. Their thick, tough flesh will be like Wellington boots if you cook it quickly.

This is when you need to make cephalopod stew. Or salad. Or one of the all-time great tapas. Please note: small squid are not suitable for this procedure.

The stewy version: cut the denizens of the deep into bite-size pieces after preparing them in the usual way. Put in a casserole or oven-tolerant saucepan with fat or oil, flavourings, and wine or stock to cover. Get it bubbling, then simmer as gently as possible; there should barely be bubbles breaking the surface of the liquid. The cooking might take an hour, so do your first bite-test at that point. It might take as long as four hours, so test again at 30-minute intervals. The good news: cooking times are fairly forgiving because the heat is so gentle.

If you're using the lovely beasts in a salad or a tapa, do exactly the same thing but with plain old H$_2$O. Drain when done. Proceed with salad. Or, for the tapa (*pulpo a la Gallega*), set them out (warm) on a platter, drizzle on top-notch olive oil, and dust with paprika and coarse salt. Embraceable tentacles. Heavenly.

SCALLOPS

Subject: scallops seared in a pan, brown without and juicy within. A commonplace on modern menus, and in chefs' recipes. One problem chefs forget to mention, however, is that it's impossible to sauté more than one portion of these beauties at home. The simple reason: they take such a short time to cook. By the time you've finished putting the sixth scallop in the pan, the first one in needs to be turned. By the time you've put in number twelve, number one is done – if not overdone.

But the dish itself is possible if you make three sacrifices. One: buy huge, incredibly expensive scallops. Two: be prepared to abuse your smallest non-stick frying pan. Three: during the initial searing, you must do nothing apart from breathe, blink, and cook.

Sacrifices accepted? Then remove the corals and dry the scallops well. Frying pan – blazing hot, filmed with oil. Extractor fan – full blast. Take a scallop in a pair of tongs. Press one flat surface on the pan till lightly brown and flecked with black spots (c., 30 seconds). Turn and repeat on the other side. Remove to a non-stick baking sheet. Repeat with remaining scallops. When they're all done, you can let them cool and then refrigerate.

Blast-off: preheat oven to 200C/400F/Gas 6. Roast scallops (top shelf) for 4-5 minutes. Watch very carefully: the instant you see expressed liquid in the tray, they're done. Serve as you wish. Cooking this way, you can easily do scallops for a crowd of 10 or even more – if you don't mind selling your house to pay for them. Penury was never so blissful..

MUSSELS

After years of cooking mussels in the usual way, in a big pot on the hob, I had a few changes of heart on the subject. One of the most important lies in the boring matter of cleaning. Of cleaning barnacles, to be precise. It seemed unnecessary to me. After discussing the subject with my friend and colleague John Whiting, a gourmand with few peers, I realised I was wrong. John removed barnacles because he thought they contributed unmentionable flavours to the dish. I let them stay because I am lazy. I tested the difference between a barnacled and an un-barnacled bivalve, and discovered that he was right.

But how to get rid of the annoying encrustations while still remaining lazy? I found the answer. Instead of scraping them off with a blunt knife, as is usually suggested, you can bash them with the head of a plastic washing-up brush. Carefully target the barnacles and whack once or twice till they crumble. The residue can then easily be scraped off. It takes some time, but a lot less than the knife routine.

Second change of heart: cooking method. The classic mussel procedure is to cook aromatics (garlic and the like) in oil or butter in a big pot, then add the mussels and liquid (usually white wine). The method is usually described as steaming, but it isn't. The mussels on the bottom get boiled, those on top steam. They cook unevenly. You can toss them, in theory, but tossing a kilo or two of mussels is about as easy as tossing a bucketful of rocks. And another thing: straining the cooking liquid, to remove the grit

released by the mussels, is a pain. And yet another thing: if you want a concentrated sauce, you have to cook down the strained liquid while the mussels sit there losing heat.

It occurred to me: why not make the sauce in advance, by cooking the flavourings with their wine and reducing it to a thick sludge? I tried it, and it works. Just follow any good recipe for mussels, but cook all the additional ingredients in a frying pan or saucepan till the liquid is reduced to just a few spoonfuls. In the meantime, clean the mussels (cue washing-up brush) and discard any that don't close up. Cook them in a pot. Strain the precious liquid, which is like pure mussel essence. Put mussels, liquid and sauce-goo in a big bowl. Eat.

But that tossing in the pot? I found some alternatives: roasting or grilling or barbecuing.

All these ideas assume that you have cleaned the mussels, discarding any that remain open. If you're going to be keeping them for a while between cleaning and cooking, keep them in water to cover – either in the sink or in a big bowl. Just before use, drain them – but no need to dry – and toss with a little vegetable oil to help keep the shells from drying out. The tossing can be done in a bowl or in the cooking pan if you're grilling or roasting.

A General Note on Cooking

Mussels can be eaten raw, as you know if you've had a plateau de fruits de mer in France. But there are few foods more horrible than an overcooked mussel. If they're not rubbery, they're leathery. The flavour goes. Avoid at all costs.

This is a particularly important consideration with dry cooking methods like those I'm proposing here. Because they take less time than the traditional steaming/boiling method, and expose the mussels to a higher temperature, the margin of error is smaller. That means you have to be vigilant. I have found that the mussels should be taken off the heat when they still look a little undercooked. But don't worry, even if you hate the idea of undercooked shellfish: the mussels continue to cook in their shells, which get very hot and retain the heat – acting as mini-ovens for their inhabitants.

A Note on Storage

Mussels have to be very fresh, and it's best to eat them as soon as possible after purchase. But if they are really fresh, they can be kept overnight. Some people say you should wrap them in wet newspaper for storage, but my investigations suggest that submersion in water works better. I bought some very fresh specimens, cooked half, and kept the rest overnight in water. The next day, they were very nearly as good as they'd been the day before.

BBQ

To cook them on the barbecue, first place them on a flat roasting rack from your kitchen. This means you

don't have to hover over the hot coals, and also ensures that they all hit the heat at the same time. They can be tightly spaced, but they must be in a single layer and lying as flat as possible. Place on the preheated BBQ and cook for anything from two to five minutes. Sorry I can't be more specific, but it all depends on the heat of your barbecue.

If you're barbecuing casually and are happy to serve mussels a few at a time, you can dispense with the roasting rack and place them right on the BBQ. If you hate the idea of losing some of the precious mussel-juice to the coals, put them on aluminium foil. This will slow down cooking but will leave you with juices to be used later (see THE BIG BONUS).

GRILLING

Grilling works fine, though I would place it below barbecuing and roasting. Leave the mussels in water till the instant you are ready to cook. When you're all set, put them in a large roasting tin or the grill pan, and preheat the grill. IMPORTANT: Set the rack so that the mussels won't be closer to the heat source than four or five inches.

Put them on the tray(s) in a single layer. It doesn't matter if they're crowded, but they mustn't be piled up. Now drizzle a tiny bit of oil on them, and toss well; if you prefer, you can do the tossing in a large bowl and then transfer to the roasting tray.

Grill the mussels for 3-5 minutes, checking them frequently once the two-minute mark has passed. Stop the cooking when they're still a little underdone. And see THE BIG BONUS for the final stage.

ROASTING

My preferred method, which I now use to the virtual exclusion of all others. Take out one or two large roasting tins and preheat the oven. The temperature should be around 180C/350F/Gas 4, though a bit lower or higher won't make much difference.

Lift the mussels out of their water and put them on the tray(s) in a single layer. It doesn't matter if they're crowded, but they mustn't be piled up. Toss with oil as in the instructions for grilling.

Put the tray(s) in the oven, near the top if possible. Set the timer for 3 minutes, and check them by opening one and tasting it. They may need a couple of minutes more, but proceed by cooking

for another minute at a time and then checking again. As with grilling, you should stop the cooking when they're still a little underdone: the shells retain a lot of heat and continue to cook the mussels. They can now be removed from the tray(s) while you deal with:

THE BIG BONUS

The juice produced by all these methods is truly wonderful – milky white, sweet and salty at the same time. To be usable it must be strained through the finest sieve in your kitchen, or through muslin or a kitchen towel. Once that's done, you can serve it with the mussels – as a dipping sauce on its own, perhaps with a bit of extra virgin olive oil or a drop of wine; or mixed in with whatever sauce you have made (if you've made one); or save it and use it as the basis for fish sauce or soup. It will freeze well. Or, if you like, you can make:

A LITTLE MUSSEL SAUCE

Cook some chopped onion or garlic in butter for a good few minutes at a very low heat. Add other flavourings – saffron, a little chilli powder, spices, herbs – if you wish. When the garlic or onion is really soft (15-30 minutes), put in a glassful of white wine and let it cook down to almost nothing. Now add a few spoonfuls of double cream and let it cook down to around half its volume. When the mussels are cooked, strain their liquid into the pot and cook for a few minutes, till the sauce is thick and fragrant.

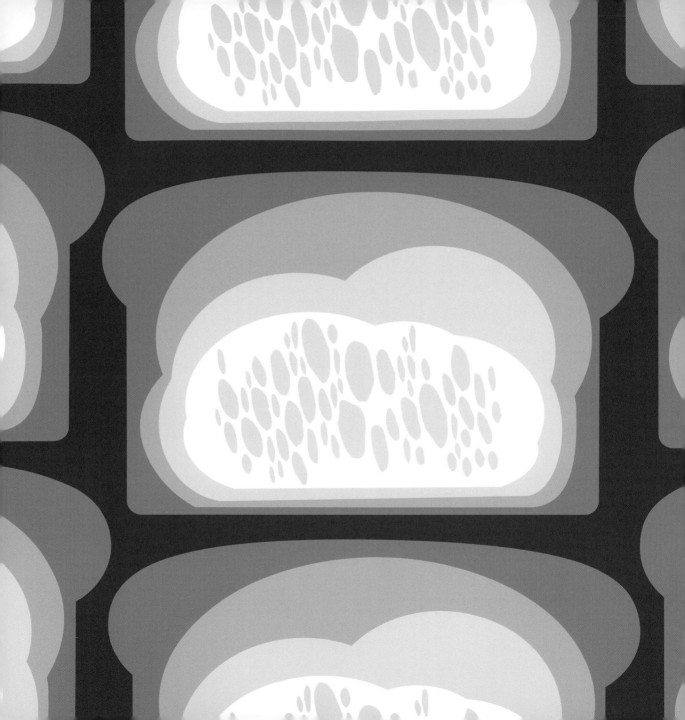

SIMPLE BREAD

Thousands of cooks convince themselves they're 'baking their own bread' when they dump ingredients into a bread machine and then go off to play tennis. They are doing no such thing. The active work in making bread by hand can be done in twenty minutes. It is no more difficult than frying a burger. It gives profound satisfaction. The results are twenty times better.

There are many good bread books around, or books on baking with chapters on bread. Three of my faves: *Baking with Passion*, Dan Lepard and Richard Whittington; *Bread: From Ciabatta to Rye*, Linda Collister; and *Bread*, Eric Treuille and Ursula Ferrigno. My specimen recipe is just a very simple basic loaf.

A FEW POINTERS

The first of which is: you don't need to knead by tipping the mixed dough onto a floured work surface. You'll save on washing up if you knead in the bowl, which works just as well.

Tip two: don't be intimidated by kneading. It is not an arcane mystery. Grab dough by one edge, lift, then push down at the centre with the heel of your hand. Repeat. Throwing it into the bowl works too, and it's fun. Single kneading taboo: don't stretch the dough too much.

Tip three: the second rise in loaf tin or on baking sheet. Most recipes tell you to cover the tin with towel and cling film, but you'll have a disaster if the dough touches them. Much better: a big bowl. There's no danger of having it stick to the cover.

Tip four: make bread fit into your schedule. If you use less yeast, or let the dough rise in the fridge, the rising will take longer. You can make the dough at night and pop it in the fridge. In the morning, punch it down and put it in the bread tin (2 minutes work). Refrigerate. Bake in the evening.

This recipe is based on one in the book that taught me how to bake bread: Martha Rose Shulman's *The Bread Book* (sadly out of print). It is the model for almost every loaf I bake myself. It makes two loaves, so you will need two 20 x 10cm (8 x 4in) loaf tins. You should try to use stone ground, unbleached, STRONG flour (higher in gluten than ordinary flour).

425ml (³/₄ pint) water
10ml (2 tsp) active dried yeast
Around 675g (1¹/₂ lb strong white flour)
5-10ml (¹/₂ tsp) salt

First step: heating the water. It must be lukewarm, which means a temperature of 35-40C (95-105F). I like to use an instant-read digital thermometer to be sure of the temperature, but your hand really is good enough once you've got the knack. Just remember that your normal body temperature is 37C/98.6F, so water that feels warm but not hot is correct. Heating the water is easiest in the microwave. Put it in the mixing bowl and then heat for anything from 30-120 seconds. If you don't have a microwave, heat the water briefly in a saucepan and transfer to the bowl.

When the water is right, put in the yeast and leave it for around five minutes – till the yeast starts to froth up a little. In the meantime, measure out the flour and the salt. Have a coffee mug or small measuring cup at the ready, and a stout, long stirring utensil such as a wooden spoon.

OK, yeast is frothing up. Now add a cupful of flour and mix it in using a few good stirs with the spoon. Add another cup, mix in, and add another cup. Scrape down the sides of the bowl to mix in crusty bits of adhering flour. Keep doing this until the dough seems more solid than liquid – the dough will feel too tough and resistant for stirring with a spoon. This should happen when you've used around 600g (1⅓ lb) of the flour. It is a sign that it is time to start kneading. Scrape down the sides of the bowl, mix the scrapings in, and get ready for fun.

As I've already said, there is no magic to kneading. Put some flour on your hands and a little more on the top of the dough. Get your fingers around the far edge of the ball of dough, lift it up, and fold/push it down on the centre of the ball. Keep doing this. As you knead, you will notice that the ball becomes more resilient and springy. If you knead for five minutes and the ball still feels wet and sticky, add a little more flour. Don't be afraid to use all the flour, but don't be surprised if you don't need to. Your aim: a ball of dough

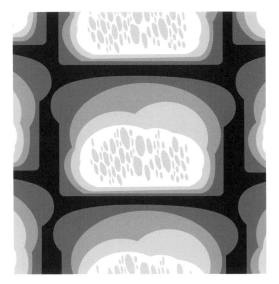

that is springy, smooth, firm and elastic.

Kneading can take anything from 5 to 15 minutes. It can be done, once the ball has begun to feel firm and resilient, by lifting the whole mass up and throwing it into the bowl. You will probably feel uncertain about it the first time you try it. After that, it will be second nature. And you will love it.

There is just one thing to watch for in kneading: too much stretching of the dough, which can lead to tearing. Without going into the technicalities too much, it's important to understand that kneading dough means forming the long strands of gluten which enable the dough to expand. If you tear those strands, the bread will taste good but will not rise properly or have the right texture. Just remember: don't pull hard on the dough. When you've done it once, you will very quickly get the feel for the right kind of handling. Careful but firm.

THE FIRST RISE

When you have that springy, smooth, firm and elastic mass, shape it into a neat ball. Don't worry if you see seams here and there. Cover it tightly with a damp tea towel (a few splashes of water will suffice) topped with a plate, or with cling film. Leave it on the table or counter, or in the fridge, until it has roughly doubled in size. At room temperature, this can take as little as 1½-2 hours. In the fridge, it can be left for 8 hours or more.

THE SECOND RISE

Once the dough has doubled in size, it has to be 'punched down' – have the air taken out by pressing down firmly all over the ball with your fist. Put a little flour on your hand first. It will still feel springy, smooth, firm and elastic. Knead again briefly. Very satisfying.

Now you have two options. One: leave it to rise a second time in the bowl. Two: form it into pieces of equal size and put them straight into the loaf tins. I usually go for option two, though a second rise in the bowl is no bad thing if you're not in a hurry. If you want a second rise in the bowl, just re-cover and leave as at the first stage.

INTO THE LOAF TINS

Whether you've done the second rise in the bowl or gone straight for the final stage, the procedure is the same. Brush the loaf tins with oil (this can be omitted if you have non-stick tins). Punch down the ball of dough, knocking the air out of it, and cut it in half using a very sharp knife and swift slashing strokes. Try not to pull on the dough.

Now pick up one ball and quickly knead it in your hands. Form it into a slab that roughly fits the bottom of your loaf tins. If one side of the slab has fewer 'seams' where two pieces of folded dough have met, keep that side facing up. Place it in one tin. Using your knuckles, press it into all four corners and make it lie roughly flat. Press out large air bubbles. Repeat with the second lump of dough. Cover the tins, ideally by putting a large bowl over each one. If you cover them with a towel or cling film, the bread may rise to a height at which it touches the covering. If this happens, removing the covering will cause the dough to sink.

BRUSHING

Brushing the top of the dough with an egg wash (1 egg with a little water) helps the crust form a nice glaze. I don't usually bother with this. If you want to, brush when you put the knocked-back dough in the loaf tin. If you wait till it's risen, the brushing may cause the dough to lose some air and make the surface look untidy.

BAKING

When it's ready to bake, the dough will have risen to around the rims of the tins. This should take around 1½-2 hours at room temperature, or around 8 hours in the fridge. The middle of the loaf should be a bit higher, but don't worry if it seems flat. When they're close to reaching that point, preheat the oven to 190C/375F/Gas 5.

If you have a baking (pizza) stone, preheat that in the oven (allow an extra 10 minutes of preheating) and place the tins on it: it will help the bottom of the loaf go nice and crusty. Put the tins in the oven, on the same shelf if possible. Set the timer for 50 minutes.

WATER

Steam helps bread form a golden crust. Put a dish of hot water on the oven floor, or spray the surface of the loaf with water once it's been baking for 10 minutes or so, or both. You can also just splash water on the oven floor a few times during baking.

TESTING

Rap the top of the loaf with your middle knuckle. If it makes a hollow, wooden-drum-like sound, the bread is done. When you hear that sound, get the bread out of the tin ASAP.

REMOVING THE LOAVES

This can be tricky. Pick the tin up and try to turn the loaf out onto a clean, dry surface. If it doesn't want to come out, run a thin-bladed knife along all four walls of the tin. If you're unlucky, some bread on the bottom of the tin may adhere to it. This is a shame, but it won't ruin the loaf.

I often put finished loaves back in the oven for a few minutes, upside down and right on the oven shelf, to brown the bottom and sides more. This is strictly optional. Not optional: leave it to cool on a wire rack for at least 15 minutes.

DISCLAIMER

Bread-making can go wrong, even for experienced bakers. This is especially true when you try to use different types of flour, large additions such as dried fruit, or complex shapes. I urge you to stay with this simple recipe while you're learning the ropes, though minor variants (adding a handful of bran for roughage, a few tablespoons of extra virgin olive oil for flavour, dried herbs for flavour, a sprinkling of coarse salt on top) can be introduced almost from the start. But if your whole bread-making life is confined just to this loaf – as 90 per cent of mine is – you will derive immense pleasure both from the making and from the eating. Even your 'failed' loaves will be delicious. I'm a lousy baker, but I always turn out good bread. By hand. My only electrical bread-baking aid: the radio.

PIZZA CRUST

We are not talking about store-bought pizza bases. We are talking about pizza dough, home made at the expense of around 15 minutes of your time (10 using a food processor) and 15 brain cells'-worth of intelligence. And then pushed and poked and cajoled into forming a thin disc. A disc which, when properly baked, is crunchy, flavourful, and a worthy foundation for your toppings.

Got that ball of risen dough? Good. First of all, flatten it gradually and gently: the dough is full of spring, and if you stretch too fast, the springs will recoil. Use fingers, palm, knuckles – anything except a rolling pin – till the dough starts recoiling. Let it rest for 5-10 minutes, then attack again. You're getting the dough to work with you instead of against you. Second point: make it thin. The thickness of a magazine might be a good target, unless they've sold lots of advertising. Too much thickness = too much stodge and too little crunch.

Final step: bake the pizza on a pizza stone, available from almost any cookware shop, or a perforated metal sheet (ditto), or an unglazed ceramic tile from a DIY shop. Ceramic options: preheat thoroughly. That dry heat will crisp the bottom of the crust better than any baking sheet ever can. And when you've crusted properly once, you will expect nothing less.

FRIED RICE

There are four essential points to remember about fried rice, and the first is not to take it too seriously. Fried rice does not rank among the essential dishes of the Chinese repertoire, even if it costs five times more on Chinese menus than steamed rice. It is viewed in Chinese families as a snack, and as something you make to use up leftover rice. Unless you have some of that commodity in the fridge, you shouldn't even think about making it.

Is that a reason to disregard it completely? Not on your life. All of us sometimes cook too much rice. If you find yourself in that position, then the other fried-rice essentials – all practical in nature – come into play. The first: you need dry rice that has been accurately cooked, the grains al dente, not sticky or clumping. Break up any little clumps by rubbing the rice gently between squeaky-clean hands. If there's moisture hiding in there, spread out the rice on a baking sheet and leave it to dry for an hour or so. Second: the rice must go into blazingly hot oil and never stop moving while in the pan. A wok is best, any good frying pan will do. And figure on around 10ml of oil per 200ml of rice. Third: while the rice is in the pan, no liquid – especially soy sauce – should get anywhere near it. Cooking time will depend on the amount of rice and the size of the pan, but it won't be much more than a couple of minutes in any circumstances, as long as the oil starts out hot (and stays that way).

How do you turn this likeable leftover into a delectable dish? By using the pan, first of all, to make a standard stir-fry. Here's an example. Assemble some suitable veg cut in small dice, around the size of a pea. Peas are a good start, as it happens. French beans, carrots, courgettes, asparagus – good places to continue. And some chopped garlic, ginger, and spring onion. Stir-fry the veg in a good spoonful of oil till barely cooked then put in a little liquid (stock and/or wine) and finish the cooking. Make sure the liquid cooks away completely. Remove, wipe out the pan,

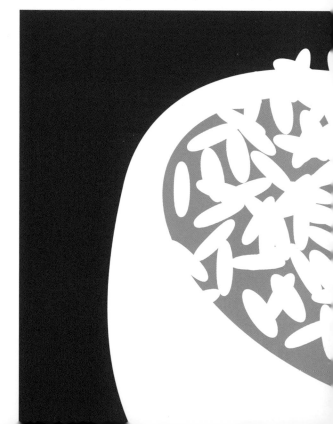

POTATO SALAD

and proceed with the rice. When it's cooked, put back the veg and stir it up vigorously for a few moments. And at this point, of course, a little soy sauce can go in – though it isn't necessary. Some sesame oil would be a better bet, used in small quantities (say 2.5ml/ ½ tsp per 200g of rice).

It isn't a masterpiece. But it's so delicious that no one will notice. As long as they don't pretend they're eating a Chinese delicacy.

You need to remember a grand total of two things to make perfect potato salad. One: use firm, waxy potatoes, such as the heavenly Jersey Royals. Two: toss the cooked spuds with any acidic or winy companion while they're still hot. That's it. Next on the agenda? OK, maybe there's a bit more to say. Reason for rule number one: hot spuds soak up liquid better than cold, and heat tames both acid and alcohol. Absorption is also the reason unpeeled spuds must be halved or sliced. Rationale for rule two: floury spuds turn to mush when they're tossed.

Done? No, one more rule: just say no to cold potato salad. Hot, warm or room temperature shows the flavours best. And maybe just one other: add oil only at the last minute. You want watery stuff to be absorbed, but the oil should be a coating. What's more, it should be oil and not mayonnaise – fine in a New York deli, but not in a European potato salad, which is the best kind of all.

OK! That's it. Except for a few optional avenues to potato salad ecstasy. After oil, vinegar/lemon, salt and pepper, try garlic, onion, fennel (seeds or fronds), dill, anchovies, bacon shreds. That's a partial list. It could go on. OK? Good. Done.

OVEN CHIPS

If there are any parents in the room who have never fed their children McCain's Oven Chips, would they please make themselves known to the Guinness Book of World Records? This excellent product – 5 per cent fat content – is a godsend when you're short on time. But the homemade alternative is cheaper, and in most ways better even if it lacks the 100 per cent consistency that you get with an industrial product. Not bothered? Then read on.

Procedure: assemble good baking potatoes, neutral oil and one or two large non-stick baking trays. Oven: 200-230C/400-450F/Gas 6-8. Peel the spuds if you wish, slice around 60-120mm ($^1/_4$-$^1/_2$ in) thick, then cut the slices into batons of the same thickness. Dry them on a tea towel and convey to a clean plastic bag. Now pour in oil, at least 25ml per potato. Close off the bag and knead, shake – anything to coat the pieces evenly. You can also do this in a bowl, mixing with your hands.

Here comes the painstaking work. Dump the chips on the tray(s) and spread them out to separate by at least a chip's width. When they're all in place, sprinkle with salt and put on a rack or racks near the top of the oven. Test after 15 minutes; 20 minutes will probably do the trick. It's not McCain's perfection, but you can eat it without guilt – whatever your age.

POTATO GRATIN

Perfecting potato gratin means solving a critical technical question: how do you soften the potatoes without leaving them too wet, and form a crust on top (and bottom, if you're lucky) which is crunchy but not dry? Numerous cookbooks present definitive answers. Problem is, they all disagree. Washing the sliced potatoes; using milk instead of cream; topping with grated cheese. The disputes are bewildering. After lengthy experimentation, I reached some conclusions which I won't abandon in a hurry.

But most of all, I reached three conclusions about the bigger picture. One: you cannot publish a recipe for perfect gratin without specifying every single detail. That's why a long discourse follows. Two, good news: there are different ways of reaching gratinistic perfection. And three, better still: even when a potato gratin isn't perfect, it's still going to be the best thing you've eaten all week.

In what follows I am describing every detail of the dish as I have finally settled on making it. But I am also presenting it as a general recipe which can be adapted according to the specifics of your equipment and ingredients. Cooks have different gratin needs at different times.

The Basic Gratin

Equipment:
A shallow, heavy dish – Pyrex, enamelled cast iron, heavy-gauge aluminium or ceramic (see opposite for measurements)

A mandolin (optional)
Aluminium foil to cover the dish completely
A metal spatula

Ingredients:
1 clove of garlic
Plenty of butter OR suitable animal fat such as duck or goose fat
1-2 baking potatoes
Liquid (see below)
Nutmeg (sometimes optional)
Salt and pepper

The Cooking Dish
The ideal gratin should contain one or at most two overlapping layers of sliced potato. That means, for a baking potato weighing 400-450g, a dish with a surface area of something like 150cm square (55 square inches). It does not matter what the shape is, as long as it has roughly this surface area. For dividing the gratin into portions, however, oval and square dishes are better than round. And low walls on the dish are crucial, as you want to be able to slide in the spatula nearly parallel with the base of the dish.

Garlic
Any gratin benefits from a hint of garlic, and the best way to introduce that is by rubbing the bottom of the dish with the cut side of a plump clove. You could chop the clove very finely and scatter it on the bottom

of the dish, but it is difficult to achieve an even distribution. So: halve the garlic clove and rub the cut side(s) energetically on the bottom of the dish.

Fat

Now you need to grease the bottom and sides of the dish, and you need to grease well. Gratins always stick, but they will stick less if there's plenty of fat underneath the layer of spuds. For a dish of this size, you will need at least 15ml (1 tbsp) of fat. Make sure the butter is generously distributed; evenness is secondary.

The Spud(s)

There is endless discussion about the best kind of potato to use for gratins, and I am not going to enter into that discussion. For most purposes, the one to use is any type of 'floury' potato: anything you would use for baking. Peel the spud and cut out any nasty bits. Lay it on the chopping board, and cut off half an inch at one end; the rounded ends will not lie happily in the dish.

Slicing

The ideal thickness is around 30mm (⅛ in), but don't go nuts trying to get this exactly right. Uniform thickness is more important than precise measurement of thickness. If you have a mandolin, this is the best tool to use for slicing. If you're using a knife, use one with a thin blade as this is more likely to give uniform, even

slices. As you slice, keep thinking: I NEED THIN SLICES. When you get to the last half inch of the spud, discard it as you discarded the first. Do not wash the slices: their surface starch promotes the formation of that creamy texture.

Preheating

At this point you should preheat the oven to 200C/400F/Gas 6. Have one shelf at a point around two thirds of the way up in the oven.

Layering

A crucial step. The slices should be laid out like fish scales. Working from the outside of the dish, place one slice with its long side facing the rim of the dish. Now place the second so it covers the first by around two thirds. If you're using a round dish, this means working round the circumference of the dish. If using an oval or squared dish, put down one column of layers along one side of the dish, then place another next to it with the edges very snug; the bottom of the dish should not be visible. If there is still some dish showing when you finish, adjust the layers slightly to cover any gaps.

If you are using two layers rather than one, simply repeat the process just described.

Liquid

Now it's time to put in the other crucial ingredient: the liquid that will – in the first stage of cooking – part-boil, part-steam the potatoes, and which will blend with their starch to make the creamy goo which gives the dish much of its texture.

Let's be frank: cream is unquestionably the best gratin liquid. Nothing else gives the same flavour (a kind of nuttiness) or the same rich texture. If you want to go down this route, here are my preferred options:

100 per cent single cream
70/30 mix of single and double

You can also get acceptable results by using a small proportion of cream to a high proportion of milk – or even by using 100 per cent milk. The dish will lack richness and texture, but it will taste good and will not be quite so killing on the calorie front. Use whole milk, rather than semi-skimmed or skimmed.

Stock

Gratin Dauphinois is made with cream. The other French classic, Gratin Savoyard, is made with stock.

Stock-based gratins can be delicious, as long as the stock is good. If this suits your purposes better, do it. The measurements are the same. If you want to add richness (and follow the Savoyard principle), grate Gruyère or something similar over the top.

The Liquid Measurements

I would rather not measure the liquid by volume. It makes more sense to measure by depth: fill the dish to a depth of around one half the depth of the layers of potato. The volume of liquid needed for this can vary considerably. For the quiche dish I usually use, with a single large potato, this means, approximately 150ml (¼ pint) of liquid.

But don't follow these measurements religiously. Look at the depth. That's what matters.

Many recipes tell you to bring the liquid to a boil before putting it in the dish. This is especially useful if you want to let the seasonings infuse in the liquid, and/or if you want to speed up the cooking in the oven. It does not, however, make any difference (that I can see) to the final result.

Seasoning

Once the liquid is in, you can season. A grating of nutmeg – light dusting over the whole surface of the potatoes in the dish – is de rigueur for Gratin Dauphinois. For a stock-based gratin, it is not necessary – and would be regarded as incorrect in the canon of classic French cookery. Salt and pepper are essential: again, a light dusting of both over the whole surface.

Covering the Dish

If you are using a dish that has its own cover, use it. If not, use a large sheet of aluminium foil stretched tight over the dish. Important: the foil must not touch the spuds. If it does, the spuds will lift away when you remove the foil for the final stage of cooking.

Cooking

Put the dish in the oven and set the timer for 20 minutes. Or for 15 minutes if you have poured hot liquid over the potatoes. When the timer goes off, lift up the foil and get out a sharp knife. Stick the knife into the potatoes at the centre of the dish, and at the perimeter. Is there just a hint of resistance? Do the potatoes seem to be around half-cooked? If the answers are yes, remove the foil. If no, put the foil back on and cook for another 5-10 minutes till the answers are yes.

The Final Dotting with Fat

When the spuds are half-cooked, the foil needs to come off and you need to dot the top with little pieces of butter or with duck/goose fat if that's what you're using. You can also brush the top with double cream. The rationale is to add richness, to keep the top from drying out, and, most important, to facilitate the formation of a crunchy crust. Be generous with the fat. An approximate measurement for butter would be 30ml (2 tbsp). Return the uncovered dish to the oven and set the timer for 25 minutes – or for 20, if you have a fan oven. From 20 minutes of the secondary stage of cooking, you need to keep a close eye on things. In my oven, the total cooking time is always approximately 45 minutes but you may need an hour or more.

How to Tell When It's Done

A gratin is done when the top is crusty all over, deep-gold in parts, and perhaps touched with bits of black. The liquid is bubbling furiously, but it has reduced to a point where even the furious bubbling barely reaches the surface: you can see it from the side of the dish (if it's Pyrex or something else transparent), but not on top. And the blade of a small knife, when stuck into the gratin, goes in very easily. At this point, you need to serve it within a couple of minutes. Those minutes of resting will enable the gooey juices to retreat into the potato. After that, you start to lose something essential.

Serving

Because the crust is tough, it is easy to disturb the layers when you're slicing and serving. That's why I put a flat metal spatula among the list of needed

items of hardware. The best way of cutting into the crust is straight down. Avoid sawing, as this is the surest way of disturbing those layers. Cut the gratin into serving portions, making sure you cut right through to the bottom of the dish, then carefully lift out each portion – again without disturbing the layers. Even if you are using a round dish, as I've been doing, cut the gratin into roughly square or rectangular pieces. They're easier than wedges for slicing and serving.

A gratin of the size I describe will not feed many people – especially because it's so delicious that everyone will want to eat a lot of it. If you're feeding a crowd, it is much better to make two or more gratins rather than trying to make one with more layers.

TIMING WITH OTHER DISHES

Because a gratin can't wait, it's important to serve it with dishes whose cooking time is flexible. Timing steaks or chops will be nearly impossible unless you're a chef. Much better: a roast or a braise, especially of lamb. When the gratin seems to be a couple of minutes from being done, get the lamb etc. ready for carving; as soon as it's done, start carving. Don't keep that gratin waiting.

BELLY OF PORK

Belly of pork, one of the best yet cheapest parts of the pig, is sadly undervalued in western cuisines. We should treat belly with the heartfelt reverence of the Chinese.

Anatomically and culinarily, the defining feature of pork belly is its alternating layers of meat, fat, and connective tissue, with a lining of skin (rind) on one side. This structure leads the Chinese to call it 'five-flower' pork, in reverent reference to those layers. Look for a thin layer of subcutaneous fat, since very fatty slabs are too rich even for lovers of pork fat. The bones, if they're still in place, make slicing somewhat more difficult but help the belly keep its shape during cooking. The slab will be around 5-10cm (1-2 in thick), and thickness determines cooking times.

To roast a piece of belly, you need to remember just three words: gentleness, attentiveness, and fearlessness. Gentleness applies to the cooking heat, which should not climb above 150C/300F/Gas 2. Roast belly toughens easily, and a slowish heat makes toughening easier to avoid. But even at a low heat you need attentiveness, a watchful eye in the final stage and a sensitive finger. When the flesh side feels firm to the touch, with just a hint of 'give', it is ready.

And fearlessness? That applies to the traditional, erroneous view that pork must be cooked till well done or you'll die from trichinosis. Fact: trichinella spiralis, the nematode that causes this disease, is seldom found in pork nowadays, and is killed at 58C/137F – when the meat is still rare. Medium-rare meat,

stopped in its cooking tracks while still tender and juicy, is the target here.

So: rub the rind with vegetable oil and sprinkle with salt. Rub the flesh with spices, if you so desire. Put the slab in a roasting tin with a splash of white wine or water. Cook for 60-90 minutes, testing frequently after 60. When it's done, the skin probably won't be at crackling-point, so flash it under a moderate grill for a few minutes.

The other way to go belly-up is through braising, which takes the worry out of timing and leaves the rind as a meltingly soft sheet. Here is a specimen recipe, based on the classic 'red-cooked pork' of Sichuan province. The idea, however, is infinitely adaptable. I have also braised belly with all manner of European seasonings, and it's always great. Once you gain the same kind of familiarity, you will cook up your own variations.

Red-Cooked Pork

To serve 3-4 people

Around 500g (generous pound) belly of pork, skin on

A big knob of fresh ginger, peeled and sliced

3-4 cloves of garlic, peeled and halved

2 spring onions or a section of leek, cleaned

75ml (5 tbsp) soy sauce

45ml (3 tbsp) dry sherry or Chinese Shaoxing wine, or dry white wine

30-45ml (2-3 tbsp) brown sugar

1 piece star anise or 5ml (1 tsp) of Chinese five-
spice powder, or a small stick of cinnamon or
cassia in a pinch
Around 500ml (scant pint) light chicken stock

If you want to be kosher-Chinese, as it were, you
should blanch the pork first. I confess to never having
seen the point of this, and don't think you will suffer
by omitting it. Continuing with the kosher method,
you would brown the pork slices quickly in vegetable
oil. This too can be omitted, though you should do it
if you want the extra complexity of flavour that comes
from browning. My usual procedure: don't brown,
and leave the pork in a single piece. The taste is
milder, since less surface gets exposure to the highly
flavoured cooking liquid. If you prefer to cook it in
pieces, cut slices around 1-2 inches thick.

Preheat the oven to 150C/300F/Gas 2 if you are
going to be braising the pork in the oven.

Whether browned or un-browned, the pork or

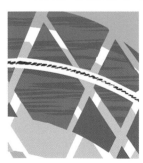

pork slices should go
into a heavy casserole
that will hold every-
thing in a single layer.
Add all the remaining
ingredients except
the stock, making
sure all the solids are
tucked in between
the pieces of meat.

Now add the stock. Note: the quantity given above is
merely a guideline. Pour it in until the liquid covers
three quarters of the height of the pork pieces, with
the remaining quarter sticking out of the liquid. If you
don't have enough stock to do that, make it up with
more wine – or even with water, though this will
dilute the cooking liquid.

Bring the casserole to a boil, then cover it tightly
and cook on hob or oven. If using the hob, employ a
low heat that maintains a steady but gentle simmer.
By either method, but especially on the hob, you need
to check on proceedings regularly. If the liquid is
cooking away too much, add more. You should also
turn the pieces every 30 minutes or so to ensure even
cooking. For the rind (skin) to cook properly, it needs
to spend at least 45 minutes in the liquid.

Cooking time: around 1½-2 hours. There is a lot
of latitude here, as already mentioned, but the pork
shouldn't cook endlessly or it will – like all braised
meats – dry out. Many cooks tend to think that
because the meat is cooked in liquid, it can't get overcooked. This is not true.

The best way to test braised belly: poke it with a
chopstick. If the chopstick goes in easily, the meat is
done. The rind should be perfectly soft, an unctuous,
melting mouthful. Sorry: no crackling here. But soft
rind is just as wonderful in its own way as the crackling of a classic British joint.

The best accompaniment: plain boiled rice. The
alternative: mashed potatoes.

BUTTERFLIED LEG OF LAMB

Leg of lamb butterflied means: boned and trimmed and split open along the internal seams so that the meat, when laid out on a flat surface, lies flat. Your butcher can do it easily; you can do it too, though not nearly as easily. It'll take an expert five minutes, whereas you will need half an hour or so the first time you try. Whichever road you travel to lepidopterated lamb, you will have before you one of the best things ever cooked on a barbecue. It can seem daunting the first time you face one, but it's easy to manage.

The key to success: view a butterflied leg as an over-sized chop, not as a joint. Though irregular in thickness, in most places it is not much thicker than a double-cut loin chop (i.e. two loin chops cut as a single piece). So conventional roasting is contraindicated. Think instead about slow, steady cooking, combining direct heat and indirect. Like open coals: start it over high temperature and then lower the heat, by moving the meat away from the coals, moving coals away from the meat, or covering the BBQ. Or in the oven: sear under the grill, then finish at medium-high (around 180-200C/350-400F/Gas 4-6). Or do the whole thing under the indoor grill, as long as you can control its heat effectively at low temperatures. Whichever method you use, butterfly cooking time has a curious tendency to last around 45 minutes. It needs some attention, though not much more than you would need for roasting a leg of lamb in the normal way.

Is that all? Well, you'll probably want to marinate the thing for 24 hours – but you probably guessed that already. This all-purpose marinade can be varied ad infinitum, Oils: extra virgin or sesame. Liquids: wine or vermouth. Acid: sherry vinegar, citrus or verjuice. Plus shallots or spring onions, spices, chillies, whatever herbs seem right (e.g. tarragon for fish, rosemary for lamb) and I have to say that garlic is always a welcome ingredient in a marinade of this kind. Slicing? Couldn't be simpler: just slice on the bias from any direction. Guarantee? You'll love butterflies once you've made their acquaintance.

CRACKLING

HAMBURGERS

Under normal circumstances, the crackling on a piece of pork will be more popular than the pork itself. This uniquely British foodstuff is easy to create using what is now (after long experimentation) my favourite technique. Oven temperature: flexible, but 180C/350F/Gas 4 works well. Preparation: dry the rind with paper towels and then rub liberally with vegetable oil. Sprinkle lightly but thoroughly with fine salt. Roast, without basting. When the pork is done, the rind should be crunchy.

But crunchy takes time, and with smaller pieces of pork, time's in short supply. That's when you need the labour-intensive crackling kick-start: pre-cooking the rind in an oiled frying pan, holding the pork down with tongs so the skin starts to crackle before the meat starts cooking. If you're kick-starting pork chops, you can hold two or three in the tongs. Slowly turn them to crackle the whole strip, and figure on 10 minutes for complete coverage. When they're fully crackled, do the proper cooking under grill or in the same pan (if it's big enough).

Small pork joint? Just get the crackling process started in the frying pan, cooking long enough to let the rind begin its bubbling and stiffening. It will reach its conclusion in the oven, and can be salted before it goes in. Either way, it's more work than roasting a full-size joint. But no sacrifice is too great for good crackling. For further discussion, see A Roast for Two (page 47).

Hamburgers are junk food only when made with junk. When made right, they're heavenly. And making them right begins with careful selection of the beef. This means, almost inevitably, that you can't just pick up a packet of minced beef from a supermarket shelf. What you need instead: individually select slabs of braising steak with a fat content of around 10-15 per cent. Get them minced through the medium plate. A supermarket butcher, if there is one where you shop, should be willing to oblige. If they aren't, go to a good butcher – they need your business just as you need their quality and expertise.

If you want to season the meat before forming the discs, you are welcome to do so (though I personally add seasonings through garnishes). A little salt, a larger amount of black pepper – obvious choices. Some people like chopped onion in the mix, and I do not oppose it on religious grounds, even if I prefer the purity of plain beef. Onion also adds juiciness, which is extremely useful if the beef is on the lean side. But if you are of the onion school, I beg you to soften them first in butter or oil: a burger doesn't cook long enough to make alliums shed their sting. Let the softened onions cool completely before mixing in the meat.

The essential prep: forming thy patties, the make-or-break step on the path to Hamburger Heaven. Thickness can be 15-40mm ($\frac{1}{2}$-$1\frac{1}{2}$ in), as long as it's uniform. Neaten up the edges, but take account of the all-important patty-forming principle: don't

RACK OF LAMB

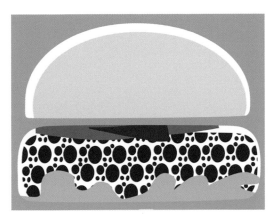

A rack of lamb – or carré d'agneau if you only speak French in the kitchen – seems like an extravagant thing to cook for ordinary evening meals. And so it is. But it's also one of the best and easiest. These six-eight cutlets are among the choicest bits of a lamb. You just need to remember the numbers twenty and five to cook them perfectly.

To start with: preheat the oven to 200-220C/400-425F/Gas 6-7, and set a heavy frying pan over a medium heat. If the pan can't go into the oven, have a roasting pan at the ready. When the pan is hot, put in oil just to film it. Salt the rack on the skin side, then put it in the pan with salted side down. (Extractor fan on, please.) After five minutes or so (magic number), the skin will be medium-brown; but if you're a stickler for uniform cooking, check it midway through, and hold it as needed to brown any bits that are not getting browned. (This is only for the fastidious; I don't usually bother.)

Brown? Then take the pan off the heat. Turn the rack over, or transfer it to the roasting pan with the skin side up. Season with spices or herbs, your choice, and slam it into the oven.

Twenty? That's the time needed in the oven, give or take a minute or two. Five? That's the resting time, minimum, as well as browning time. And also the extra time the rack will need if you choose to dispense with the preliminary browning. Either way, your rack will be irresistible. Five. Twenty. Delicious.

squeeze hard or the burgers will be too dense. The discs should hold together, but there should be some air in there.

The cooking: grill or fry? I'll take high-heat frying any day. Get a thick, uncoated pan (or griddle) hot enough to make a drop of water sizzle away instantly. Turn on the fan. Season the top(s) with salt, then slap onto the pan with salted side down and press briefly with a spatula. Don't even think about moving them for a minute, till the surface is seared. Turn when the first side is deeply browned.

When are they done? Let your fingers judge. Approximate temporal values for medium-rarity: 15mm, 90 seconds a side; 40mm, 2½ minutes a side. Digital values: very springy = rare; slightly springy = medium rare; rock-hard = ruined. That's it. Cue burger bun. Cue ketchup.

ASPARAGUS

The hoops through which some recipes make you jump for asparagus! £100 purpose-built steamers – buy now! Peel the stalks! Bundle up with string! It's all wasted money and effort, honest. Try this instead.

The prep: wash the spears and cut or break them at the point where green turns to frog-belly white. Wash. Lay your hands on any big, deep pan that will hold the spears easily with a few inches of H_2O to spare. Add the water in question, make it boil frantically, then salt well.

The cooking: slip in the spears and wait 1-2 minutes for the water to regain the boil. Now start timing. Some recipes want you to boil those green fingers for 10-12 minutes. Bah! Test stiletto-type spears after 4 minutes, Nellie the Elephants after 5. To test: lift out a spear, slice a section off the end, munch. If it's ever-so-slightly al dente, you're there. If not, keep cooking and test again after 60 seconds. I promise it won't take more than 6-7 minutes if there's plenty of boiling water.

There are alternatives to boiling. The best, by a long shot, is roasting. Preheat oven to 200C/400F/Gas 6. Trim spears. Wash them and shake off excess water. Lay them in a roasting pan, in a single layer or near enough, and pour in 30-45ml (2-3 tbsp) of extra virgin olive oil per 450g of asparagus. Roll pan to coat spears and sprinkle with coarse salt. Roast for 12-15 minutes, removing when they're slightly browned, very slightly crunchy at the tips, and easily penetrated by a knife.

This is the way I cook asparagus 95 times out of 100. It's just as good as water-based cooking if you're serving spears in a salad-y assembly. Cool suggestion: roasted peppers, shreds of prosciutto, thin wisps of spring onion.

Not satisfied? Well, some people like to grill or barbecue asparagus – and so do I, though it takes a bit more trouble. Brush the spears all over with oil. Grill till they're deeply browned (sublime crunch and flavour), which will signal that cooking is nearly complete. After brushing with oil and turning, they will need just another 1-2 minutes, to give a total cooking time in the vicinity of 12 minutes.

Still not satisfied? Consider stir-frying. Trim, wash, cut spears into 5cm segments. Heat a wok or frying pan with a generous squirt of vegetable oil till it's smoking, and stir-fry with a little salt for a minute or so, till the spears start taking on a little colour. Turn heat down to medium-low, add a little water, cover pan. Cook for another 3 minutes or so, aiming for al dente. Toss with lemon juice. Serve.

Eat asparagus every single day when it's in season. But please: do not waste your money (or litres of aviation fuel) on imports in January.

BARBECUED VEGGIES

Barbecued vegetables are drop-dead delicious. But the casual approach of some recipes masks a disturbing reality: they are often trickier to cook than meat, especially if you're grilling several varieties in one go. If you don't believe me, look at the exemplary recipe for Charcoal-Grilled Vegetables – time consuming, and almost forbiddingly precise – in Marcella Hazan's *Essentials of Classic Italian Cooking*.

Worth the effort? You bet! Just remember four things. First, and most important: barbecued veg taste as good when warm or room-temperature as they taste when hot, so they should be cooked before anything else goes onto the coals. Second: use a moderate heat, and take pains to avoid excessive blackening. You're looking for gentle cooking and just a few wisps of charred material. Third, don't get fiddly. Cut everything into large pieces that facilitate lifting and turning, or just leave them whole. And no skewers: too hard to turn. Four: brush every single bit of surface area with plain vegetable oil.

Many vegetables take well to the coal-fired treatment: courgettes, aubergines, fennel, peppers, summer squash, small onions (quartered), big mushrooms, and smaller mushrooms on skewers are all prime candidates. They will still take an age to barbecue, especially if you're cooking a lot of them. But they will repay the effort. Which is all that counts.

If you need to feed vegetarians and omnivores together, a grand platter of grilled (or they could be roasted) vegetables, doused with a garlicky dressing,

could be your salvation. Pleases both camps equally, enables you to place the whole meal on a single serving vessel and eliminates the need to coordinate cooking because everything cooks at its own speed.

The drill runs something like this. Prepare some vegetables and get them grilling under (or barbecuing over) a moderate heat. While they're cooking, prepare another load. When the first batch is done, remove it to a platter and start cooking the second. Repeat this process until you've cooked all the vegetables. You can cook more than one type at a time if this suits you, though this calls for more care and attention.

Want a little sauce? Then try grilled tomatoes in flavoured oil. Ingredients: cherry tomatoes, extra virgin olive oil, finely chopped garlic, herbs (optional) of choice. Put them in a metal dish and grill, barbecue or roast just until the tomatoes are starting to fall apart – 5 minutes or 15 minutes, depending on the heat. To serve, gently squash the tomatoes so their gooey juices mingle with the oil.

This fragrant oil/tomato mush binds the vegetables together. Slop it on an hour ahead of time, with regular spooning-over, or dump it on at the last minute.

BEETROOT

Everyone knows two things about beetroot. One: it's used to make borscht. Two: it's horrible. Or wonderful. People love it or loathe it, and there's rarely any wishy-washiness between those extremes. As a member of the beet-loving faction, I would like to add a few more points to your certainties. The most crucial of which concern preparation, not cooking.

Why preparation? Because as soon as you expose the interior, you expose your hands, chopping board and cooking vessels to nearly-indelible staining. Solution? Postpone the exposure by cooking the bulbs with the skins intact. First of all, buy small beetroot – no bigger in diameter than the length of your index finger. Trim away all but an inch or two of the leaf stem – saving the leaves, if they're in crisp, lively condition, for a salad – and leave the rodent's-tail-like tip intact. Wash the beetroot with alarming thoroughness – a really good scrub, though not brutal enough to break the skin.

You're now ready to cook that beetroot in the best of all possible ways: by roasting it. Oven temperature's flexible, and may be determined by the temperature you're using for other things, but something in the vicinity of 200C/400F/Gas 6 is ideal. Put the bulbs in a roasting pan, with a bit of space between them, and rub the skins with oil. This keeps them from going excessively brittle and therefore makes peeling easier. Start testing after an hour, and don't be surprised if they need up to fifteen minutes on top of that. Test as you would a baked potato, with a small, sharp knife or a metal skewer.

When the beetroot is cooked, it is ready for action. Meaning: back to preparation mode. As soon as they're cool enough to handle (five minutes should do it), put them on a plate (not a stain-magnet chopping board). Don a pair of rubber gloves if you have some, to keep your hands from turning purple. Carefully peel, rub and pick away the skin, taking care to remove every single scrap. As they're done, transfer them to another plate.

When skins are sloughed off, you're ready to rock. Roll the purple globes into a pan with some lightly cooked garlic or onion, toss in the hot oil for a minute or two, and serve as a side dish. If you want to turn them into a salad, cut them into slices or batons. But beware: the knife should be a table knife, preferably serrated, rather than a kitchen knife which would be dulled by contact with the plate. Toss with a vinaigrette, accessorising with any variety of allium, and either use immediately or leave in the fridge for up to three or four days. And you may, of course, use them to make borscht. But you knew that one already.

BRAISED VEGETABLES

BRUSSELS SPROUTS

Hang on a sec. Aren't we supposed to steam vegetables, or stir-fry them? Surely braising makes them soft, rather than modishly al dente. Well, you may treat food as a vitamin supplement if you wish. But then you'll miss out on one of humanity's great inventions. Willing to have a go? Then choose celery, leeks, Belgian endive (chicory), fennel, carrots, cauliflower. Clean and cut into manageable pieces. Get some stock ready. All set.

Preheat the oven to 140C/275F/Gas 1 or thereabouts. Put the veg in a heavy, lidded casserole or a baking dish, and pour in stock to come halfway up the vegetables. Salt, pepper, lots of butter on top. Cover on, or wrap aluminium foil round the baking dish. Into oven. Baste regularly. Timing: 40-90 minutes, depending on the depth of the veggies in the pot. When they're done (easily pierced by knife-tip), they can be left for a while (gentle reheating at blast-off) or served immediately. Either way, a crucial step: before serving, place pot over high heat and boil down the cooking liquid to a thick, syrupy consistency. This concentrates the flavour and makes a voluptuously buttery 'gravy.'

Optional flavourings? You pick. Garlic, spices, dried herbs, bacon, a drop of wine. Just remember that reducing act. And the basting. Simplicity itself. Al dente – it's not always the vegetal ideal.

Sprouts can be dull and dire. But it doesn't have to be this way if you liven them up a little. Which means, first of all, buying little green Brussels cannonballs: hard, tight, no trace of brown or yellow. Slice off their bases, but ignore the old idea of cutting a cross in the base. Codswallop, pure and simple.

First-choice cooking method: steaming. Takes longer than boiling (and needs a big steamer) but yields a less watery, more uniformly cooked sprout. Whichever method you use, remember the cardinal rule: overcooking = death. If you're going to bathe the little dudes in butter and serve without further ado, cook until just soft enough to eat. If they will have to wait before serving, undercook slightly (faintest hint of crunch at the centre) and reheat gently in the butter. Gentlest stirring, too: they moult their outer leaves easily.

The better way to ennoble sprouts involves a two-step cooking process, parboiling followed by a quick braise. Described below, and a small price to pay for banishing Brussels boredom.

If you're going to treat sprouts to further cooking, you have to make sure they're not overcooked in the initial parboiling (or par-steaming or microwaving). Test them when you think they'll be around 75 per cent done. When a small, sharp knife is inserted, it should move easily until it reaches the centre, at which point there should be some resistance. It's hard to say how long this will take, but as a rule of thumb:

Boiling: 5 minutes
Steaming: 10 minutes
Microwave: depends on quantity of sprouts and power of machine (sorry)

When that stage is reached, drain the sprouts. You don't need to 'refresh' them (i.e. run under cold water), which can make them shed outer leaves and might leave them soggy. But spreading them out in a single layer so they cool quickly is a good idea. This can all be done hours in advance.

For the final cooking: braising or pan-braising. The two methods are similar, but one is done in the oven and the other on the hob. The hob is fine for smaller quantities, the oven is better for large. I am giving a basic recipe plus variations for ordinary braising, with just a brief description of the hob-top option. All the variations can be played on the hob.

Braising

This is a particularly good method at Christmas because the oven is on anyway, and the sprouts will adapt well to whatever oven temperature you're using. The recipe here is just a specimen, very classic and delicious but easily modified to incorporate whatever ancillary seasonings you wish to use. Some suggestions are given at the end.

BRAISED BRUSSELS SPROUTS WITH CHESTNUTS

To par-cook the chestnuts, simmer them in water or (much better) stock until they're barely soft enough to eat (around 35-45 minutes). You can cut them in pieces if you prefer. A roasting tin will serve as the cooking vessel, but a heavy gratin dish or shallow casserole is better. The quantities are for a sizeable Christmas group but can be changed as needed. And of course, you can leave out the chestnuts if you wish.

900g (2 lbs) par-cooked sprouts
225g (8 oz) peeled, par-cooked chestnuts
1 small onion, finely chopped
Lots of butter
Chicken stock to moisten the sprouts (optional)

First of all, sweat the onion in some butter. That is to say, cook it gently without colouring till it turns translucent. Remove from the heat. Put the onion in the baking dish and add the sprouts and chestnuts, shaking the dish to distribute everything evenly. The sprouts should ideally be in a layer no more than 2 deep. If necessary, use 2 or more pans. Season with salt and pepper, dot generously with butter, and cover with the pan lid or with aluminium foil. May be prepared in advance to this point.

When you're ready to cook, drizzle in a little stock (if using) and re-cover the pan. Cook in a moderate oven (around 180C/350F/Gas 4) or at the bottom of a hotter oven for around 20 minutes. As long as the butter isn't burning, the sprouts can safely be ignored while you rush round the kitchen.

Variations:

DUCK FAT AND SHALLOTS

Even more delicious. Use duck fat instead of butter to sweat the shallots, 3-4 of them, finely chopped. But dot with butter, not duck fat!

A LA CRÈME

Pour in 100-150ml of whipping cream (or double cream slightly diluted with milk) and use somewhat less butter.

WITH SPICES

Sprinkle on around 10ml (2 tsp) of ground mixed spices: cinnamon, nutmeg, cumin, coriander.

CHINESE FLAVOURS

Instead of the onions in the master recipe, use a small handful of the holy trinity of Chinese cooking: ginger, garlic and spring onions.

Pan-braising

For this you need a large, heavy frying pan or a flame-proof roasting dish. Proceed in exactly the same way, but use a little more liquid as it cooks down faster. The sprouts need to be in a single layer or they'll cook unevenly, and stirring causes major leaf-shedding. If the heat is very low and the pan very thick, this method can take around the same time as oven-cooking. If not, figure on around 10 minutes instead of 20.

CAESAR SALAD

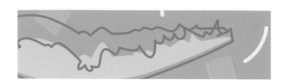

When Frank Sinatra sang Cole Porter songs, he often tweaked the words to suit his phrasing. Porter finally griped to the great singer: 'If you don't like the words to my songs, why do you sing them?' Caesar Cardini might say something similar to many of the chefs who claim to serve Caesar salad. If you don't like salad, why do you make it in so many stupid and unnecessary ways?

For the record: A Caesar salad does not contain chicken, salmon, prawns, or… aw, don't get me started. It does contain Cos lettuce, croutons fried with garlic in the oil, chopped anchovy fillets, and freshly grated Parmesan. You put the lettuce in a big bowl. Then you make the dressing.

The dressing does not contain mint pesto, balsamic vinegar, or… there I go again. Shut me up, will you? The dressing does contain extra virgin olive oil, which is tossed with the lettuce. Then you add half as much lemon juice, salt and pepper, and the remaining solid ingredients. Finally you break in a coddled egg (boiled for 1 minute, timing from when the water returns to the boil). You toss it well. You sprinkle on a good handful of Parmesan. You sit down. You eat.

You came, you saw, you conquered. Ignore imitations. They're the bottom, not the top.

COLESLAW

You know why I love coleslaw so much? Because I agree with the great American cookery writer James Beard that 'It is as old as cabbage and has known many different versions – and strangely enough, practically all of them are good.'

You can make perfect coleslaw just by shredding or chopping cabbage and mixing it with mayo and seasoning. But why stop there? Some carrot and onion – sure thing. Or even a grated apple – but no other fruit, puh-leeze. Nor will I reach for my Uzi if you add dill, caraway, or poppy seed.

The crucial cole-culations are dental resistance and choice of dressing. Crunch-lovers should shred, toss and eat tout de suite. Softies should steam the cabbage briefly, or make the slaw well in advance so acid and water can do their work. I prefer it with the cabbage well softened, but this is a personal matter.

On the dressing front, it's a choice between bottled mayo and something fancier. A 50-50 split of mayo and sour cream is good. So is vinaigrette with a little mustard. But a cooked dressing is my first choice if there's time. Here's the recipe.

COOKED DRESSING FOR COLESLAW

This is based on the recipe in James Beard's *American Cookery* (1972), which in turn is based on the recipe in Fanny Farmer's *Boston Cooking-School Cookbook* (1896). It can be made in a heavy-bottomed saucepan, but I strongly recommend a double boiler. Mr Beard says this quantity will sauce around 450g of cabbage, and I don't exactly disagree. But some people like runny coleslaw, some like it drier. The sauce will keep, refrigerated, for several days.

    20ml (4 tsp) sugar
    A pinch of cayenne or chilli powder
    25ml (5 tsp) plain flour
    Yolks of 2 eggs
    A good knob of butter, softened
    175ml whole milk
    50ml (3 tbsp) red wine vinegar
    5-10 ml (1-2 tsp) English mustard

Mix the sugar, cayenne and flour in the bowl that will go into your double boiler. Season well with salt and pepper. Now whisk in all remaining ingredients except the mustard, in the order in which they are listed. In the meantime, get the water heating in the bottom of the double boiler.

Put the bowl over the heat and start whisking. Do not stop for more than a few moments while the mixture is cooking. Cooking will take something like 15 minutes, and the sauce is done when it's thick enough to coat the back of a spoon. Strain into a clean bowl to eliminate any lumps, and whisk in the mustard. Use the larger amount if you want a hotter result, the smaller if you want just a mustardy accent.

You now have two choices. One: refrigerate till needed. Two, if you want to speed up the softening of your coleslaw: toss with the cabbage immediately.

CUCUMBER SALAD

A cucumber is a fine thing, but I find – maybe it's just a weak jaw – that if you eat enough of it your teeth start to lose their will to live. The steady crunch, crunch, crunch does them in. And I'm not the only one who thinks so. In cuisines that really know their cucumbers, they treat them to a softening treatment before they reach your waiting jaws. This also has the effect of drawing out water, and intensifying their natural flavour.

The treatment calls for nothing more exotic than salt, around 5ml per cuke. Peel the Freudian objects, halve lengthwise, and scoop out seeds and watery pulp with a small knife and a teaspoon. Slice thin, toss with the salt in a colander. Go away for 30-60 minutes. Return to the cukes and pat them as dry as possible with a clean towel. They are now ready for tossing with whatever dressing looks good to you.

The options? Numberless. Eastern European standard: vinegar, a little sugar, paprika, garlic. French: plain old oil and vinegar, with a little mustard. Chinese-style: grated ginger and a vinaigrette with a few drops of sesame oil in addition to the plain stuff. Herbs that love cukes: dill, tarragon, fennel fronds. Whatever the dressing, just remember that preliminary salting.

LEEKS

In the dark days of winter, we seek nourishment in cheap, soothing meals inflicting low caloric damage. That's probably why nature invented leeks. This glory of the British winter costs relatively little. It is extremely versatile. And when treated properly, it is a far better vegetable than the costly imports from the southern hemisphere that currently gobble up aviation fuel to take their place on supermarket shelves.

To get the most out of your leeks, choose them well. Huge specimens are inadvisable, tough in both outer leaves and core. A maximum diameter of around 5cm (2 in) is better; even smaller than that is fine, as long as you don't find yourself paying a fortune for insipid 'baby' leeks. Desired appearance: bright sheen in the outer leaves at the white (root) end. Undesired appearance: perceptible browning, dryness, softness, wilting.

Cleaning leeks gets some negative press, and not without reason. Sand and dirt can be taken up between the leaves at the interface of white and green leaves, and if you don't get rid of it you'll take the same particles onto your fork. The traditional prescription calls for cutting an inch's-deep notch in the trimmed green end and rinsing it under the tap while spreading the leaves. Not a terrible idea, but it makes life harder if you're going to cook them whole (the best way). Better procedure: check to determine the amount and location of dirt. If there isn't much, make that notch a shallow one. If there's a lot, consider slicing off more of the green end.

Loads of green waste sitting on the chopping board? Nil desperandum. Wash well, chop, and use with celery, carrots, garlic and herbs to make vegetable stock. Or use it as a base for roasting meat or  chicken – flavour-multiplier of distinction.

Back to the main event: those sturdy white cylinders. They perform at their peak when cooked slowly in a fair amount of oil or butter and enough liquid (stock if poss) to soften but not swamp them. A cover is needed, too. First venue for the performance: a heavy roasting dish in the oven, classic French braise. Figure on an hour or more at moderate temperature, with liquid to come around one-third up and plenty of butter. Baste regularly, but don't try to turn them once soft: they'll fall to bits. Venue two, even better: a heavy frying pan with a lid. Same specs for butter and liquid. Cooking time is shorter, c., 30 minutes, and you can watch the performance (and regulate heat) much better.

Want to speed things up even more? Slice your leeks into fine discs; messy but marvellous. If you want to make them into something fancy, serve them with shellfish; a natural accompaniment. If you just want leeks in their glory, do as little as possible.

ROASTED PEPPERS

PREPARATION MADE EASIER

Anyone can roast a pepper, and every cookbook is required by law to have a recipe for them. Extra virgin olive oil and your chosen flavourings – anchovies, garlic, capers, whatnot – dabbed on if the peppers are halved before roasting. Oven somewhere between 150C/300F/Gas 2 and 220C/425F/Gas 7. Peppers in oven for somewhere between 20 and 40 minutes. Turn them once or twice if they're being cooked intact. What else is there to say?

There is this: getting the seeds out of a pepper is one of the most depressing of kitchen tasks – the culinary equivalent of unblocking a drain, though not as time-consuming.

That's why I simplify the task with one of two little tricks. Trick one, step one: hold the pepper in one hand and a small, very sharp knife in the other. Cut all around the stem end, just below the cap, cutting through the wall of the pepper but no deeper. Step two: pull off the flesh from around the stem while leaving the stem itself in place; eat the pieces you pull off. Inside the pepper lies the exposed pith, which holds the seeds in place. Cut all round it, close to the pepper wall, without piercing the flesh. Step three: grasp the stem and gently twist and pull out the innards. The few remaining seeds will come out when you trim the pith.

Trick two: proceed through step one of the first procedure, then make a single lengthwise cut through the wall of the pepper. Work your thumb into the cut,

at the bottom of the pepper, and gently pull the two halves apart. Most of the seeds will remain attached to stem and pith, and can easily be cut out with a small, sharp knife.

The pepper can now be roasted whole or in halves, leaving no seeds to tweezer out when the pepper is a slimy mess. So much easier, dontcha think?

SALADE FRISÉE

If you're thinking of making a salad with frisée lettuce (curly endive) using industrial-grade, thinly sliced, watery, plastic-wrapped bacon, move along please. This simple dish, one of the masterpieces of simple French cooking at home or in a bistro, can only succeed with superior bacon cut to a decent thickness. Think of slices around 6-12mm ($^1/_4$-$^1/_2$ in) thick, rind ripped out, in shreds of around the same thickness. For a normal-size head of frisée, you will need around 150g of bacon. Wash the lettuce and dry comprehensively. Assemble 45-60ml (3-4 tbsp) red wine vinegar, a dainty splodge of mustard if you wish, and a large salad bowl.

And now think about your schedule. This salad must be served at precisely the moment when it's finished. You have to wait for it; it will not wait for you. Ninety per cent of the work can be done in advance, but the final burst should occur while the guests are salivating at the table.

Done thinking? Then put the bacon in a heavy frying pan with 30ml extra virgin olive oil and let it sizzle at whatever pace suits you – slowly if you have time, medium if you're in a hurry. It doesn't greatly matter as long as you don't (a) let them cook to a splintery crunch, or (b), just as important, allow their rendered fat to brown too deeply. Blackened fat will taste awful. If the bacon is very lean, add extra oil. When the bacon is just cooked, crisp and brown, turn the heat off.

While the bacon cooks, employ a clever trick I picked up from Mireille Johnston's *The French Family Feast* (out of print): warm the salad bowl by sloshing it with hot water. (The microwave is good for this.) Dry the bowl when it's warm, and fill it with lettuce torn into large but manageable pieces – of a size that means you'd have to cut them in half to get them in your mouth without embarrassment.

OK, folks: it's showtime. Heat the pan to warm the bacon thoroughly. Scatter the shreds and all the oily, unctuous pan juices over the leaves. Add the vinegar and (optional) mustard to the pan and swirl to mix well. Pour over the salad and toss well while still warm. Useful tip: if the salad is hard to toss, the cause is friction; which is caused in turn by too little oil; which is remedied by pouring in another spoonful. Salt and pepper. And now to the table, please! Your guests are desperate.

Salade frisée can be made even more wonderful in several ways. Garlic-rubbed toast, made from a good baguette. Snipped herbs on top, especially chives. Poached or boiled eggs. But you'll have a barrel of bistro fun even without them. Simple food doesn't get any better than this.

VEGETABLES IN VINAIGRETTE

If you crave a summertime meal that can be prepared well in advance and is guaranteed to raise oohs and aahs from every corner of the table, look no further than a platter of vegetables en vinaigrette. This is what everyone ate before the world spurned France in favour of Italy, where platters of roasted veg serve a similar purpose. For my money, the French version is just as good. And a hell of a lot easier.

Procedure: make a court bouillon, which at its simplest is just water, a few dried herbs, peppercorns, some celery or fennel seeds if you have them, a good dose of salt and a larger dose of wine vinegar. Boil them up for 20 minutes or so; lift out the solids. Then add vegetables, one at a time for accurate cooking. Top choices: leeks, mushrooms, cauliflower, celery,

broccoli and its variants. Cooking times: anything from 3 to 20 minutes. As they're done, drain well and remove to a large platter.

The crucial points for perfection? Simple. Just remember not to overcook, or undercook. Drain really well when removing from the court bouillon and again before serving. (Tip the serving platter so the water runs down to one end, and scoop it out with a spoon.) Make the vinaigrette a dressing of pungent distinction, and pour it over the veg 20-30 minutes before serving. Spoon it over a few times while it's waiting, and again just before serving. So easy. Main course (served with lots of crusty bread) or side dish (served with just about anything). Pleasure on a platter.

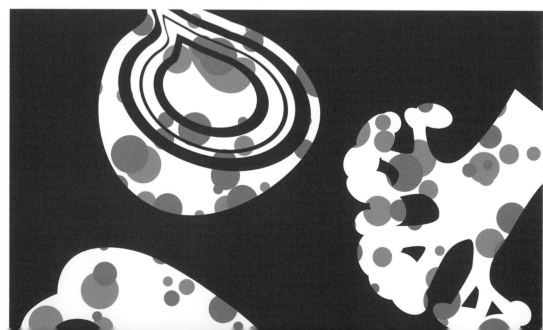

SERIOUS ONIONS

Pressed for cash? Eager to eat something delicious? Consider the onion. Too many cooks do too little with these beautiful bulbs, the cheapest and least fattening and most versatile ingredients in the kitchen. They have a dual nature – sharp and pungent when raw or lightly cooked, sweet and mellow after long application of heat – which makes them perfect for mindless, unattended oven cooking. And they invariably astonish first-time visitors to their simple but serious forms.

In the very simplest form, the bulbs need no preparation at all. You take one, of medium size (around 250g/½lb), and put it on aluminium foil or on a baking tray. You pop it into the oven, around 180C/350F/Gas 4. You leave it there for an hour or so, till a small knife penetrates easily. That's it. Serve it on a separate plate and consume by peeling and tearing off the scorched, papery skin. Revealed: a soft, yielding mass of lightly caramelised sweetness, needing nothing more than salt and pepper (and optional blodge of butter) to create the perfect accompaniment for any simple meat dish. Needless to say, this dish can be cooked for ten people as easily as it's cooked for one.

If that just seems too easy, the 180C/350F/Gas 4 oven is the home of other oniony approaches worth following. These call for a little more care in preparation and cooking, but not much more. Approach two: quarter the unpeeled onions and put them in a baking dish. Quick splash of water, quick brush with oil, salt and pepper, cover with foil. Into the oven for 30 minutes or so, till they seem around half cooked, then

remove the foil and let them cook (with one or two bastings) till slightly blackened and fully soft (another half hour or so).

Still too easy? My final suggestions require a whole minute or two more of preparation. Peel and slice around 3mm (⅛in) thick. Put the slices in a buttered or oiled baking dish, and dribble in water, wine or stock to cover by around half. Salt and pepper. Aluminium foil cover. Cook as in approach number two, adding more liquid if necessary once the cover has come off. Timings should be around the same. Basting is essential, to keep the slices on top from drying out. You could use this version as a topping for a baked potato, maybe with grated cheese on top.

And if you really want to push the boat out, turn the slices into onion crumble. Mix fairly coarse breadcrumbs with half their volume of good extra virgin olive oil. When the foil comes off, sprinkle them all over the onions. No extra liquid. Bake till the crumbs are golden. Very serious winter warmers. But with risible expenditure of time. And money.

THE PERFECT...

TASTELESS TOMATOES

Most tomatoes taste of nothing except in summer and the earliest part of autumn. (And if you buy tomatoes without paying attention to where they're from they won't taste of anything at any time.)

But let's say it's December and you're craving the real tomato flavour. If that's the case, I've got an idea inspired by a procedure described by chef Leigh Say of the exceedingly wonderful Bell Inn at Skenfrith in Monmouthshire. Say makes oven-dried tomatoes at the end of the day, when he shuts off the kitchen's volcanically hot oven. Method: core and halve the tomatoes, sprinkle with chopped garlic, dried thyme, and salt and pepper. Put on a baking sheet, drizzle on extra virgin olive oil, and leave in the oven.

Recipes from a restaurant kitchen always need adaptation for home cooking. When messing around at home, I adapted it using two approaches. One: put the tomatoes in the oven when you're finished cooking whatever it is you're cooking. Repeat the operation when the oven goes back on. The cooling-cooking cycle won't hurt them a bit. Two or three cycles should finish them off, which in this case means cooking the tomatoes down to around 10 per cent of their raw size.

Two: roast with the oven at its lowest temperature overnight, or for 16 hours, or as long as it takes to reach that 10 per cent figure. Either way, store the toms in the fridge with their oil. They will keep forever. And bring a little bit of summer sunshine into your wintry kitchen.

ODDS AND ENDS

BLINI

Every New Year's Eve I ring my beloved amigo Randolph M. Ostrow of Brooklyn, New York, who is invariably preparing to cook his standard 31/12 meal of blini. Blini (singular: blin) differ from ordinary pancakes in two respects. They're made with yeast, and the eggs are separated. Both these differences give them an inimitably airy texture which makes other pancakes look lifeless.

What's more, blini seem to work out regardless of which proportions you use of the ingredients. Ready reckoner to make around 25 blini: 250g flour, 3 eggs, 800ml milk. Some of the flour should in theory be buckwheat, though don't shed tears if it's unavailable. More important: dissolve the  yeast (say 15ml) in half the milk, heated till it feels warm. Add egg yolks and a little sugar, plus half the flour. Mix. Let it rise till volume's doubled. Beat in the remaining milk and flour, plus a little melted butter. Another rise, overnight if poss. Just before cooking, whisk the egg whites to stiffness and fold in. Fry in standard fashion. Serve warm.

Good blini don't need caviar, though they won't grumble if it's supplied. Smoked salmon – fine. Crème fraîche or sour cream – heavenly. Or just good butter, and a toast to the New Year. Or just a good evening, if it isn't a special occasion.

FAKE PICKLES

Making pickles – yes, I know. This is for people lucky enough to have time on their hands and sensible enough to spend a lot of it in the kitchen. True pickle-making calls for washing and sterilising of glass jars, for large quantities of vegetable matter and time to prepare them, and for even larger quantities of storage space. That's why humankind invented fake pickle-making, a much easier story in every respect. And an incredibly impressive addition to any summertime meal.

To make fake pickles, all you need is a few cheap ingredients and (sometimes) a refrigerator. Two methods will serve for all occasions, and the fast one is easier.

Fast one: slice an onion very thin and put it in a non-reactive bowl which will hold the slices easily. Put in a little salt and toss well, then put in acid – lemon juice or wine vinegar – and toss again. Flavour it as you wish – herbs or spices; toss again. Just two tricks to remember here. First: put in enough acid to bathe the onions generously, aiming to leave a good-sized puddle at the bottom of the bowl. Second: toss the mixture regularly, every fifteen minutes or so. It will be edible after one hour and at its best after 2-4, when the acid has turned the onions from crunchy and sharp-tasting to al-dente soft and pleasantly mild in flavour. No fridge needed. You can do the same thing with cucumbers or tomatoes (peeled and seeded) or with very thinly sliced courgettes, if you are so inclined.

The second method calls for more foresight, and a little more work. Based on a Chinese method for pickling vegetables, it illustrates – like so much of the best cooking – the transformation of pre-industrial necessity into gourmandising delight. To put plan into action, boil salt in water (around 30ml/2 tbsp per litre) just to dissolve the NaCl. In the meantime, shred a smallish cabbage and 1 or 2 large carrots; slice a few cloves of garlic; and assemble your chosen seasonings. A sliced chilli is a killer here. Put them in a bowl or a plastic tub. When the salt is dissolved, pour on just enough water to cover the vegetable matter. Stir to distribute the flavourings, leave to cool. Cover. Stick in the fridge.

You are now at the beginning of a long, leisurely process of fake-pickling. Once or twice a day, stir the cabbage etc. thoroughly to let the bits at the top become the bits at the bottom, and vice versa. After 24 hours, the pickles will be just about edible. But 48 hours is a better minimum, and the pickles will keep happily for a week or more. Flavour mellows, texture gets denture-pleasingly soft. It's that easy. None of the hard work, all of the fun.

THE PERFECT...

TAPENADE

You can make tapenade, one of the greatest pleasures of eating in southern France, with olives, capers, olive oil, herbs, anchovies and garlic. After long consideration, however, I have decided to lop the final two items off that list. Reason for conversion: a discussion with M. Rémy Pierre, oléiculteur and tapenade-maker in Octon, in the Languedoc. And a taste of his product, naturally. He says: 'Tapenade comes from the Provençal word *tapeno*, which means caper. It contains three ingredients: olives, capers, oil. No garlic, no anchovies.' M. Pierre momentarily forgot about the herbs (herbes de Provence in his case), but the point remains.

There is no intention here of entering a gastro-theological debate. My endorsement of the Pierre line on tapenade arises from two considerations: an eagerness to make the dish available to vegetarians, and a certain knowledge that simple tapenade can be extended in use by adding the other ingredients at a later stage.

So, to make purist's tapenade: first buy good olives, preferably from a specialist supplier who buys direct from France or Italy. Scrape and pinch and cut the flesh off around 275g (10 oz) of them. Black olives will yield a stronger, earthier taste; green will taste more of pure olive, and that's the one I personally prefer. You will have your own preference. Either way, process the flesh in a food processor till it takes on the form of rough chunks. Add 45ml (3 tbsp) of capers, well drained of brine, and a generous pinch of herbes

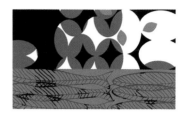

de Provence (or thyme, if that's all you have). Process to chop finely. Now add around 60ml (4 tbsp) of the best extra virgin olive oil you have. If you want a really fine paste, you can try transferring the pulp to a blender before adding the oil – but this is arduous work, and most people wouldn't bother. If you want more sharpness, add capers. More unctuousness needed? Add more oil.

What do you do with the stuff, apart from smearing it on toast? Put a dab on a plate next to plainly cooked fish or lamb or poultry. Stir some into plain rice, or add it to a tomato sauce destined to crown a bowl of pasta. Serve it as a dip with raw vegetables or breadsticks, or whisk it into a vinaigrette. Almost anything you can eat, apart from ice cream or brownies, will benefit from the addition of tapenade.

And what about the garlic and anchovies? Look, it's a free country – and plenty of people with better taste than mine believe that they're tapenade essentials. For the quantities above, blend in a clove of crushed garlic and a couple of anchovies. Your tapenade will be sharper, more pungent, much saltier and more complex. And extremely delicious, though not necessarily better than the simpler version I've come to prefer. But again – it's a free country.

THE PERFECT...

BARBECUE SAUCE

You want to make barbecue sauce? Look at any of the books by Steven Raichlen, the king of BBQ writers. But if you look at any good recipe, you will find that all have three common characteristics. One: they're

thick. Two: they have a sweet-sour balance. Three: they are of a fine texture. This is not an accident. It arises inevitably from the way BBQ sauce is used. If you follow these three principles, you can use almost any flavouring you want.

Why are they so important? Thickness is obvious: the meat has to be coated and stay coated during cooking. If the basting mixture is too liquid, it will run off. Fine texture is needed for the same reason: chunks in the sauce will run off, but not necessarily before they've burned from the BBQ fame. Sweet-sour? Easy: sugar not only adds thickness, it also caramelises during cooking and thus contributes both flavour and crust. And if you use sugar, you want acid sourness to balance.

You can make BBQ sauce just by simmering tomatoes with sugary stuff and vinegar plus flavourings of your choice, then sieving them to get the bits out. But there's sauce and there's sauce. I ate one at the wonderful Zuzu restaurant in Napa, California, that knocked my socks off. I offer their recipe herewith. No one who has ever eaten it registered a complaint. Not to my knowledge, anyway.

ZUZU MOROCCAN BARBECUE SAUCE

The green peppercorns may be dried or in brine. The lavender and serrano peppers may be hard to get hold of but are worth seeking out to make this outstanding recipe to the restaurant's specifications. Most herbs and spices can be found at The Spice Shop, 1

THE PERFECT...

CREAMY SALAD DRESSING

Blenheim Crescent, London W11 or by mail order from their web site www.thespiceshop.co.uk

Makes 450-675ml
450ml ketchup
450ml rice wine vinegar
450ml water
450ml honey
125ml soy sauce
15ml toasted coriander seed
7.5ml toasted cumin seed
7.5ml whole cloves
50g fresh ginger, sliced
3 cloves garlic, peeled and crushed
15ml cardamom pods
15ml green peppercorns, drained (if in brine)
15ml black peppercorns
7.5ml ground nutmeg
5 pieces star anise
2 sticks of cinnamon
225ml lime juice (or lemon if necessary)
3 serrano peppers (or 1-2 smaller chillies), split
    in half
15ml dried lavender flowers
½ a large bunch of fresh coriander, well cleaned

Combine all ingredients in a large stainless steel pot. Bring to the boil, then reduce heat and simmer slowly till 'the consistency is thick and "syrupy".' Strain and chill. This will keep in the fridge for months.

I know, I know: salad is healthy. But occasionally, everyone deserves to eat salad dressing that's as fattening as brownies. These politically incorrect items are a speciality in my native USA, despite our reputation for nutritional purity. Many Americans don't trust a lettuce leaf unless it's coated in saturated fat.

Result: most modest restaurants offer several creamy options, such as Ranch, blue cheese and 'creamy Italian.' Sometimes the nutritional police get their way with low-fat alternatives, but this is for wimps. When you want creamy, you want calories.

Think of CSD as a vinaigrette in which the oil is supplanted by mayo and sour cream. Mayo-cream proportions: tweakable. Greek yoghurt: good low-cal stand-in for some of the sour cream. Use less acid than is normal in vinaigrette, adding sharpness with alliums, herbs and maybe a little soy sauce or Worcester sauce.

The CSD deity is Green Goddess Dressing, invented in San Francisco in 1923. Want to worship at her throne? Here's a recipe. It's the food of the gods. And if you try it, I promise not to report you to the nutritional police.

GREEN GODDESS DRESSING
This was created at the Palace Hotel in San Francisco in 1923, to celebrate the opening of William Archer's play The Green Goddess. It was originally made for a dish of artichoke bottoms filled with shrimp, chicken, or crab. The quantities of nearly all ingredients can be

adjusted to taste, but it's important to have a high proportion of greenery to sour cream/mayonnaise: 75-100 per cent by volume.

> 3-4 spring onions or 5-6 shallots
> 1 or 2 good handfuls parsley, preferably the
>   flat-leaved type
> 4-5 sprigs fresh tarragon
> 3-4 anchovy fillets, well drained of oil
> 225ml mayonnaise
> 100ml sour cream
> 15-30ml lemon juice
> 15-30ml white wine vinegar
> Salt and freshly ground pepper to taste

If using spring onions: top and tail, then cut into short lengths; use both white and green. If using shallots: top, tail and peel; cut in half if very large. Pinch off the stems from the parsley and tarragon. Put these ingredients in a blender or food processor with the anchovies, and process till very finely chopped. Now mix in the mayo and sour cream, either in the machine or by hand.

Finally, add the lemon juice or vinegar. Start with 15ml of each and add more if you like. Season with plenty of black pepper and salt used sparingly (because the anchovies are salty). Allow the dressing to relax for at least an hour or so before using so the flavours can get to know and love each other. The dressing will keep in the fridge for a week or more, as long as the fridge is properly cold.

SALSA VERDE

The term means something in both Italian and Spanish; we're speaking Italian here. Rough translation: a condiment that makes the mouth water and the heart leap up. Ingredients, imperative division: parsley, anchovies, garlic, capers, acid, extra virgin olive oil. Ingredients, optional division: we'll get to that in a moment. To make a few spoonfuls of salsa verde, you need (approximately) 1 large handful of parsley, 1 clove of garlic, 2 anchovy fillets, a dessertspoon each of capers and acid (vinegar or lemon juice), and two spoons of oil. Those measures are not scientific: vary at will.

What is not open to debate: texture. Salsa verde should be neither puréed nor chunky but a kind of gritty sludge. Think chunks the size of rice. It's do-able in a food processor – light hand on the on-off pulse button, please. By hand, chop each ingredient separately – takes time, but so does painting a fresco.

Salsa verde is one of those fundamental preparations, like mayonnaise, where you learn the basics and then decide whether to take it further. If you decide in the affirmative, the single most common addition is mustard. (This is not considered optional by either Marcella Hazan or Anna del Conte, and God I hate to disagree with those two.) Other thoughts: basil, mint, chilli, olive. Me, I stick to the basics. And to careful texture-control, the make-or-break parameter in the pursuit of salsa nirvana.

PESTO

ROAST GARLIC

Making pesto is easy. Getting the right ingredients is hard – though some-what less hard at summer's end, when your garden (or farmer's market)

may boast lorry-loads of basil. Two of the other ingredients need a bit of care whatever the time of year. Easy: rock-hard garlic and Pecorino and/or Parmesan.

Hard: pine nuts and olive oil. Most food outlets sell them, but they have to be the right stuff. Pine nuts: Anna del Conte's *Classic Food of Northern Italy* stipulates that they be 'large and smooth, of a creamy ivory colour, and without any darker patches.' Oil: what Italians call 'dolce' (i.e. sweet and smooth). Do your research.

Any self-respecting Italian cookbook will urge you to make pesto with a mortar and pestle. Sorry, for me it's a food processor. As in: wash and dry leaves. Weigh them. Use around 60ml oil, 1 small clove of garlic and 15g pine nuts for every 30g of basil. Put in the food processor with a pinch of salt. Process till the mix resembles coarse green sand. 50ml grated cheese. Mix. Done.

Got a lorry-load of basil? Make pesto without cheese and freeze in small pots (add cheese when you serve). Enough for just a few servings? Get the pasta cooking. I'm on my way.

Here's my favourite way to eat roast garlic: the whole head, served as a side dish/condiment. Easy in principle but the execution has some tricky variables, so it follows down below for those who want the full, smelly Monty. For now, a simpler method. Software: whole cloves, separated but unpeeled, and extra virgin olive oil. Hardware: a heavy roasting pan that will hold the cloves in a single layer.

Right, let's get roasting. Spread the cloves out in the pan and toss in enough oil to coat generously. Now put in a good splash of water, which will keep the garlic from cooking too fast. If you want, you can add herbs (thyme and rosemary are tops). Cover the pan, using aluminium foil if the pan lacks a lid.

Ideal numbers: oven temperature 150-180C/300-350F/Gas 2-4, cooking time around 30 minutes. But since no one turns on the oven just to roast garlic, you can adapt time and temperature to suit your main dish. Just watch the cooking carefully. Don't let the skins go too dark – excessive browning turns garlic from sweet to bitter. Test by squeezing a clove: it should come out of its skin easily and have a lightly toasted colour. Ideal eating: straight from the oven, but room temperature is fine. Mmmm factor: off the scale.

ROAST GARLIC – THE DIRECTOR'S CUT

This is my preferred way of roasting garlic, with two alternative methods. But note: the flavourings inside the 'tent' can be varied more or less endlessly; see the note at the end for a suggestion or two.

You can take just about any simple dish and make it more impressive by planting a roasted head of garlic next to it. And it doesn't need to have power enough to stink out the whole house. Best starting point: fairly young garlic, very fresh; one large square of aluminium foil per head; extra virgin olive oil (not your best stuff).

First comes the he-man's method, for those who like a powerful garlic aroma and well browned flesh. Method: slice off the top of the head so the individual cloves are exposed. You are aiming just to cut off the tips of the cloves, which is somewhat tricky. Use a very sharp, thin-bladed knife, and angle the head so its tip is resting on the chopping board. Hold the bulb firmly with your free hand and make the cut with the knife parallel with the base of the bulb.

Now put the main part of the bulb on the foil, base down. Drizzle on a little extra virgin olive oil and put the cap back on it as neatly as possible. Drizzle on more oil, being generous with it. (The oil will taste great, and is a kind of sauce for whatever else you're eating.) Now, be careful: wrap the foil around the head loosely, so it forms a tent rather than a sheath. This is essential to prevent sticking and give the garlic plenty of steam heat during cooking. If you wish, you can put on a splash of water before closing up the tent; this moderates the oven's heat and gives more steam, which is a good thing.

Oven temperature? Aim for 150-180C/300-350F/Gas 2-4. Cooking time? Around 30 minutes. But let's be realistic: no one turns on the oven just to roast garlic. You can adapt time and temperature to suit whatever else you're roasting. If you're using a higher heat, put the garlic on a shelf near the bottom of the oven.

A cook's tip for testing for doneness. This is difficult to do visually because you don't want to unwrap the tent – too messy to reassemble, and you would probably lose some of the olive oil (not to mention the momentum of the steam). It's much better to use your ears to test for doneness. Namely: when you hear the sound of energetic oil-bubbling inside the tent, chances are the garlic is done. Don't leave it for more than 5-10 minutes after you hear the bubbling or the garlic may get too brown and therefore bitter.

Sensible person's preference: if you want the fragrance without the gross-out effect on breath and palate, simmer the heads in plenty of water till they're semi-soft – 20-30 minutes. Take them out, drain well, then proceed with the method described above. Except that: slicing par-cooked garlic is a serious pain in the neck. If you're using this method, it might be easier not to do the decapitation trick. Just do the wrapping instead, and cook the garlic for a shorter time – c., 15 minutes instead of c., 30.

With both methods, it is imperative that you not overcook the garlic. Much better to serve it warm or even room temperature than hot but overcooked. Overcooking will not only make it bitter, it will also harden the garlic instead of giving you soft, mushy pulp that can be squeezed easily out of the papery husks.

Note: flavourings can be added to the garlic in its tent. Use dry white wine, any herb that comes to hand, or a small piece of lemon. I admit, however, that I prefer the garlic in its naked glory, with just the by-now heavily scented olive oil.

GRILLED CHEESE SANDWICH

Anyone who doesn't like grilled cheese sandwiches should stop reading immediately. You may call them toasted sandwiches if you like. You may add adornments, such as tomato or bacon. As long as the double act of crisp bread and melting cheese makes you smile, you're OK. And if it does, here's a solution to what can be a tricky problem.

Problem: the sandwich needs to cook long enough to melt the cheese fully, but not so long that the bread chars. Unmelted cheese: wrong. Blackened bread: horrible. Solution: don't grill the sandwich. Fry it. Spread both pieces of bread with butter on one side, then place very thinly sliced cheese (plus adornments if you're using any) on the un-buttered side of one slice. Top with the other slice, buttered side up.

Next stop: non-stick frying pan over low heat. Fry sandwich on one side till well browned, then turn and repeat. Cooking minutes: up to ten, plenty of time to turn cheese into a bubbling blanket of bliss. Too long to wait? Not for something so delectable. Tips for adornment? De-seed tomato; pre-cook bacon, and cut into shreds for easier chomping. Tip for a surprise? Add a little tuna with mayo. This is known in the USA as a tuna melt, and it is improbably delicious.

As for the choice of cheese, which some people get remarkably wrong: the only thing you need to remember is that hard cheeses melt better than soft. Brie, Camembert and their ilk are wrong. Cheddar, Lancashire, Cheshire are the lines along which you ought to be thinking.

LARDONS OF CONVENIENCE

Vegetarians: an apology. What follows leaves you out in the cold. Bacon cannot be described even by the inebriated or the delusional as a member of the vegetable kingdom. To be specific: lardons, rind-less shreds. A lardon is the omnivorous cook's magic wand. Just point it at food and you turn prose into poetry, brass into gold, wool into cashmere. I am seriously proposing that you keep a supply of them on hand at all times.

Preparing lardons begins, needless to say, with good, dry-cured streaky bacon, sliced to a thickness of around 5mm ($^3/_8$ in). Remove the rind, leaving on as much fat as possible. Yes, as much as possible. If you're going to worry about a few extra grams of fat on a rasher of bacon, you might as well eat tofu. Rind removal: easiest with a pair of sharp scissors, but do-able with an exceedingly sharp knife. With rinds removed, you can now snip or slice the slices into the required shreds, which should have something as close as possible to a square section (i.e., like a matchstick). If you're chopping with a knife, don't stack more than a couple of rashers: the pres-

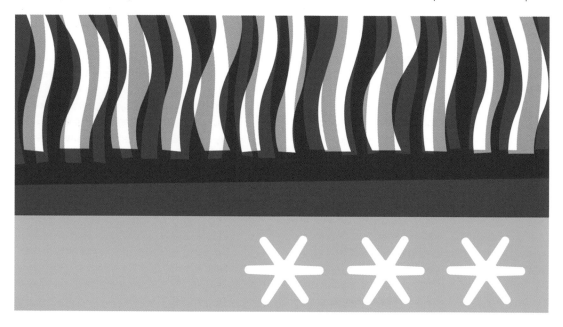

sure of the knife will make them stick together.

Preparing lardons ranks somewhere between dusting and laundry in the hierarchy of interesting household chores. Quasi-pain-relief? Do a large batch and freeze them, in one of two forms. First form: packed into small plastic bags and tied tight. Second form, and even more flexible: individually blast-frozen à la Perfecto. Lay the shreds in a single layer on a baking sheet; try not to let them touch but don't weep if they touch a little. Slide into the freezer. Freeze hard. Pop shreds off sheet and, working quickly, stuff them into a plastic bag. Seal. Into freezer. Voila: a bagful of lardons that can be painlessly extracted in quantities from a few to a few hundred. And believe me; sometimes you just want a few.

You can also stock up on lardons by pre-cooking them in large quantities. Location: your biggest frying pan. Heat: moderate. Urgent demand: do not colour them deeply, and do not let them get crunchy. This can take twenty minutes or more, with regular stirring. Done? Tip the pan so the fat runs down. Transfer the lardons to a sealable plastic tub and the fat to a different tub. Cooled and sealed, they will both keep in the fridge for a couple of weeks. Yep, shelf life's shorter than with frozen. But I bet they'll be gone before you notice any drop-off in quality. Add these filaments of pleasure to anything: rice, veg, chicken, baked spuds, blah blah. The recipient will always taste better. The consumer – you – will feel like a million bucks.

LEMONADE

How hard can it be to make lemonade? Pretty hard, if you go by the number of duff glasses I've been served in my years of drinking the stuff. Pretty easy, if you pay heed to three simple principles.

Principal principle: buy good lemons. This is not as easy as it sounds, since there's no hard-and-fast rule for judging a lemon by its cover (which is all you have to go on). Best bet: buy one, cut it open with your trusty pocket knife (which you carry at all times, like me), and have a look and a suck. Juicy flesh, good taste? Buy a bag of the lovely globes. If you have access to unwaxed citrus, and if they are not dry or shrivelled, buy those.

Secondary principle: do not over-sweeten. Lemonade should be tart first, sweet second.

Tertiary principle: use the zest. It has a flavour that's different from (and arguably better than) the juice. If the lemon is of the waxed persuasion, wash it thoroughly in hot, soapy water. Slice off thin pieces of peel, chop them into pieces as small as a grain of sand (or thereabouts), and macerate in the sugar-water.

Measurements? Not strictly necessary, but rule of thumb: 15g sugar and 150ml of water per lemon. Dissolve sugar in water and macerate them zesty bits. Strain. Add juice. Chill. Tall glass. Lots of ice. Who said there ain't no cure for the summertime blues?

THE PERFECT...

TARTE TATIN

The Tatin sisters' famous apple tart is one of those dishes with an undeserved reputation for difficulty. It's actually easy to get right if you collar a sound recipe and remember three vital points.

First is the right equipment: I recommend the Tarte Tatin tins manufactured by Silverwood or a heavy frying pan which you can put in the oven. Cast iron, plain or enamelled, is classic, but thick aluminium (like the Silverwood pans) is just as good. Anything thin is useless.

Second: use lots of apples. The fruit collapses as it cooks down, and the last thing you want is a tarte that looks shrunken. Peel, core and quarter or halve them, and pack so tightly into the pan they'd suffocate if they had lungs.

Third, and crucially, remember that Tarte Tatin is cooked twice. First thing in the pan is the sugar and butter, which you can do in two different ways. One is to cook on their own to make caramel, melting and stirring until the mixture takes on the colour of coffee with a lot of milk in it. The other is to put the apples in immediately and cook fruit, sugar and butter together, basting regularly. You'll also get good results with both methods, but with the second you can't control the caramelising process so well. Either way, it can be done on the hob or in the oven, or by a combination of methods (start on hob, finish in oven). Baste the apples regularly with the pan juices throughout this stage, and important: don't stint on time. If this takes half an hour, that's thirty minutes well spent.

If you've done everything peachily to this point, the rest is easy. Leave the pan to cool a bit if you're nervous about handling hot metal or don't feel comfortable about your pastry-handling skills. Plop on the rolled-out pastry, either rough puff or shortcrust (and

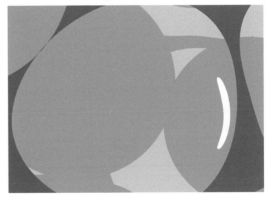

homemade if you want good results; see pages 18 and 17). Half an hour or thereabouts in a hot oven should get the apples bubbling and the pastry brown and crisp. Put a large plate over the pan and, holding it firmly in place, turn the pan over so the tortilla settles neatly on the plate. Nudge errant bits of apple into place. Serve warm, with vanilla ice cream on the side if you feel like it. That's it.

Looking for recipes? Online, consult tsa.co.uk/tatin.htm or tarte-tatin.com.

SHORTBREAD

PERFECT CUSTARD

I vividly remember the first time I tasted homemade Scottish shortbread, one of baking's greatest (and simplest, hooray!) creations. A perfect vehicle to get novice bakers rolling. But do you want to get tips on making it from someone named Ehrlich? Naah. You want tips from someone named Mackenzie, and I've got her: Aggie Mackenzie, formerly the associate editor of *Good Housekeeping*, and one of the most

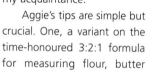

feverishly fanatical bakers of my acquaintance.

Aggie's tips are simple but crucial. One, a variant on the time-honoured 3:2:1 formula for measuring flour, butter and caster sugar respectively. She talks about 9:6:3, and replaces 2 parts of the flour with cornflour for a lighter, crumblier texture. Two, don't fill the sandwich tin right out to the walls: 'the dough needs to sit shy of the sides by about 1.5cm' so it can expand without bumping against hot metal. Three, prick the dough all over with a fork, making sure you go all the way through to the base of the tin.

Oven temperature: between 150-200C/300-400F/Gas 2-6. Cooking time: 30-35 minutes, and watch carefully at the end. Excessive browning, which tends to happen quickly, is our enemy. Final word of advice that can only come from someone whose surname isn't Mackenzie: even if your shortbread isn't perfect, it's going to taste great. And it will only get better, especially if you listen to the Divine Ms M.

Hang on a sec, which custard are we talking about? Is it custard sauce (a.k.a crème Anglaise)? Set custard as in trifle, crème caramel, or the pies thrown in circuses? Or the various crèmes of French pâtisserie? To tell the truth, I'm not sure myself. But it doesn't matter, because all custards are essentially the same thing: eggs (yolk, whole or a combo), heated with milk until the mixture thickens. The principal difference between one kind and another is how (and how far) you thicken it. For classic custard, to be used as a sauce, the approximate measurements: 300ml of milk (around half a pint), two eggs or one whole egg and one yolk, around 45ml (3 tbsp) of sugar. Plus a vanilla pod, split in half, or a dainty drop of vanilla extract.

For all custards, of whatever name, you can't screw things up if you remember the three C words: cool, cosset and curdle. Cool is the temperature you want, whether you're baking (as in crème caramel) or simmering (as in crème Anglaise). Cosset is the key to cool: snuggle an insulating barrier between custard and heat source. On the hob, a double boiler or a bowl placed over (not in) simmering water. In the oven, use a heavy dish for the custard and put it in a bain marie: a larger pan holding H_2O only. This means the mix never heats far above 100C/212F, whatever temperature the oven is set to.

And curdle means disaster: what happens if you forget the other C words. Pay them due heed and your custard will be silky-smooth. Far too good to throw at a clown.

THE PERFECT...

LEMON CURD

I don't condemn anyone who feels that life is too short to make jam, marmalade, and other breakfast-table confederates. But one toasty treat is easily essayed by the time-and-patience-starved, and its name is lemon curd. This creamy wonder requires little skill and few resources. It is essentially just a very sweet lemon custard. And the basics of the custard method apply.

Approximate measurements, for the smallest quantity worth making: 75g (3 oz) butter, 250g (10 oz) sugar, 3 lemons, 3 eggs. Melt butter with sugar over (not in) simmering water. While you're waiting for the melt, wash the wax off the lemons (unless they're unwaxed) using really hot water and a clean brush charged with your chosen washing-up liquid. Rinse mercilessly, dry, and grate the zest into the bowl. Caution: use a really fine, sharp grater (a finest-toothed Microplane is ideal), and take care not to remove any of the bitter white pith. Halve the lemons, squeeze in their juice, and keep waiting for melt-down. You don't need to dissolve the sugar completely, as some recipes say; just dissolve it enough to make whisking the mixture a doddle. Take the bowl off the heat and leave to cool for a few minutes. If it's too hot when the eggs go in, you're at risk of the dreaded curdle.

Now: bowl back over water and put in the eggs, lightly beaten and strained. Caution: use a coarse sieve, as fine mesh won't work. Whisk egg into sludge thoroughly, and step back for a few minutes of

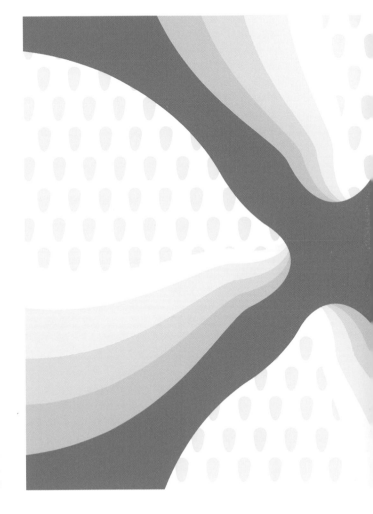

CRUMBLE

anxious hovering. Why anxious? Because when heat gets near beaten eggs, curdling threatens. And curdling is death to lemon curd as it is to all custards; perfect smoothness is your aim. As eggy sludge heats up, whisk it. As it starts to thicken, whisk it non-stop. Watch for bubbles around the rim of the bowl, a telltale sign of advanced cooking. Don't stop whisking. After 12-20 minutes, when the liquid is thick enough to coat the back of a spoon, you have lemon curd.

Decant into a fascistically cleaned jar or plastic tub. Cool. Cover.

Thirty minutes too much for you? Then microwave your curd, using a method I've adapted from Sue Lawrence's *Scots Cooking*. Melt the butter, sugar and lemon in the miraculous box (1-3 minutes, medium power). Leave to cool for a few minutes, then strain in the eggs and whisk thoroughly. Put it back in for a minute, remove, whisk it senseless. Another minute, whisk again. Keep doing this, a minute at a time. It should be done after 3-4 minutes, though precise timings will depend on the power of your microwave.

On hob or in microwave, it's so easy. Not a sterilised jar in sight. Keeps for a week or two – if you can resist the temptation to eat it morning, noon, and in bed.

Jane Grigson calls crumble a 'very good tempered' dish; the description is spot-on. Crumble accommodates slip-ups as graciously as any dessert of my acquaintance. And it's one of the best – but you already knew that. Apple. Pear. Peach. Apricot. Blackberries mixed in. Any fruit that can be baked can be crumbled.

Crumb ecstasy resides in a large proportion of crumb to fruit. That crunchy topping is what everyone really wants. You must accommodate them.

How to do it? First: weigh your fruit, then figure on around a third to a half that weight of topping ingredients (flour, butter, almonds, sugar). Second: have a dish of the right dimensions. Too small and the crumb will be soggy-bottomed. Too large and the crumb will cook before the fruit. Ready reckoner: for crumble made with 900g of fruit, try a 20 x 30cm baking dish and a topping made with 100g each of flour and butter, 50g of ground almonds, and 75g of sugar. If you increase the total weight of the topping by 25-50 per cent, you will probably make everyone very happy. Temperature: 200C/400F/Gas 6. Time: 30-40 minutes.

The ideal accompaniment is custard (see page 114). Any variety of cream will do just as well, especially if it's crème fraîche. And if you're using a preponderance of apples, some people will thank you for throwing in a handful of raisins – soaked for twenty minutes in hot water – before the baking begins. How much more accommodating can a dessert get?

CRÈME BRÛLÉE

BREAD AND BUTTER PUD

Crème brûlée, a.k.a Cambridge burnt cream; everyone's favourite dessert. Rich custard cream and brittle caramel lid which cracks when rapped with the spoon. Easy part: the custard (see page 114), but make it well in advance and pour into ramekins or another suitable serving dish so it has time to get really cold in the fridge. Tricky part: the caramel.

Making the caramel in a pot and then pouring it on is one solution, but I can't control the thickness or evenness that way. I prefer to fire the sugar after it's sprinkled on the custard. Some people say they get good results under a domestic grill, and God bless 'em (the liars). Chez nous, brûléeing calls for a blowtorch. Source: kitchen suppliers if you wish, but a hardware store is a lot cheaper. Method: as follows.

Make sure the custard is very cold and completely dry on top. Dust with just enough caster sugar to hide the custard – think of a layer around as thick as a 20p coin. Get the blowtorch blowing at full strength, then blast away at close range. The idea: shock the sugar, melting it to deep mahogany before the custard realises there's heat in the vicinity. Tip: start with the flame trained on the far edge of the dish, so you don't blow sugar around too much. Tip: you may need to practice before you get this technique right. Best tip of all: practice a few times on sugared banana slices to get your flaming technique spot-on. Practice makes perfect – and you can eat the banana afterwards. As a matter of fact, banana brûlée is so delicious that you may just decide to stop there.

Bread and butter pudding, which ranks among the simplest of the world's great desserts, takes around ten minutes to prepare. The ingredients cost a pound, if that. It is almost impossible to bodge beyond repair. You just need to approach it as a sweet gratin, ensuring softness within and crunch on top. Towards those ends, two tips.

First, the gratin needs to be well and truly wet before you start cooking. In practice, this means nothing more than soaking the ingredients – bread buttered on one side, raisins or sultanas if you like them – in a sweet custard made of whole milk, eggs, cinnamon and sugar. Don't stint on the soaking time: it enables the thick custard to permeate every cavity of the bread. (Which should be white, and of good quality.) An hour is the minimum. It can sit for longer if you keep it covered in the fridge. And make sure the liquid covers the bread initially; add more milk if it doesn't.

Second: cook gently. A bain marie – baking dish in a roasting tin filled with hot water reaching to the top of the custard – is the perfect way to proceed. Low temperature, e.g. 150C/300F/Gas 2. Long cooking, e.g. 1½ hours. Resting time – absolutely essential – of around 20 minutes. Comfort food with few peers. True happiness.

THE PERFECT...

CLAFOUTIS

Clafoutis, from the Limousin, is one of the easiest of baked desserts: a thick, sweet batter baked with cherries, prunes or fresh stone fruit. You make the batter, prepare the fruit, put fruit in buttered baking dish and pour in the batter. Leave it to relax for a while, then bake for around 45 minutes. Easy or what?

There's hardly anything more you need to know, apart from two important tips. Important beyond belief: don't over-beat the batter. The protein in the flour will open up to form long, elastic strands which make things tough and chewy rather than soft and yielding. Easy solution: beat the batter just enough to mix, then strain into the pan through a sieve and press lumps through with a spoon. Important within reason: know how sweet your fruit is. Even properly ripe

peaches, apricots, cherries etc. can vary greatly, and you need to make allowances when adding sugar to the batter. Simple solution: taste one (duh).

Which fruit? Cherries are tops, though you will have to decide between leaving the stones in (traditional) and taking them out (royal pain in the butt). Un-stoned cherries hold together better, and make for good spitting contests. I'd place apricots and plums in joint second, peaches and nectarines joint third. Needless to say, anything larger than a cherry should be halved and de-stoned: the stones aren't nearly as good for spitting contests. If using halved fruit, place it in the baking dish (well buttered) with cut surface down.

Final consideration: size of baking dish. This will depend on how many people you're cooking for, but you'll need something at least 20 x 30cm (around 8 x 11in) to feed six. Rough measurements at this size: 4 eggs, 50g (2oz) flour, 50g (2oz) sugar (or more if you wish), 600ml (1 pint) milk, pinch of salt. And about 500g (generous 1 pound) of fruit, plus a fistful of double cream for optional extra richness. Let the batter relax before baking, and you relax about temperature: anything in the general vicinity of 180C/350F/Gas 4 is A-OK.

Clafoutis is at its best warm, though room temperature will do. Cosmetic warning: it will rise during baking to create a sumptuous pillow, but deflate as it cools. Don't worry: the taste will be there. Which is to say, delicious in the extreme.

BETTER THAN BRANDY BUTTER

Here is the perfect recipe for brandy butter. Take around a pound of butter, half a pound of sugar, a good slug of brandy and a smidgeon of lemon juice. Put them in the bowl of a food processor and let the blades rip till everything is perfectly smooth. Put the blend in an old cottage cheese tub, clip the lid on, and drop the tub in the rubbish bin. No one will miss it. If brandy butter didn't exist, no one would bother to invent it.

This is a purely personal view, of course, though not one that's unique to me. Others agree with my basic points on brandy butter, namely that (a) it tastes terrible and (b) it's strange to hurl such a calorie-dense weapon at a calorie-dense target like Christmas pudding. And it isn't necessary. A light custard sauce (crème anglaise) goes much better with the festive Black Hole that is Christmas pudding.

And I've learned a lower-cal version that's better still. The knowledge comes from Sally Schneider's *A New Way to Cook*, one of the three or four truly original cookbooks of the last decade, and it's a real winner. Schneider has experimented at almost unimaginable length with new ways to shave calories from old favourites without sacrificing quality. Here is her pared-down custard, more or less as she describes it.

The recipe begins with arrowroot, a starch made from a plant native to the Caribbean; use cornflour if you need to. Measure out 225ml (8fl oz) of whole milk and remove 15ml (1 tbsp) to a mixing bowl. Mix in 5ml (1tsp) of arrowroot and stir till it's dissolved.

Pour the remaining milk into a small, heavy saucepan (and I really mean heavy, as the pan will be used for cooking the custard.) Split a vanilla pod, scrape out the seeds, and put seeds and pod into the pan. Bring to a gentle simmer.

In the meantime, whisk one egg yolk and 45ml (3 tbsp) of caster sugar into the starch mixture. When the milk has reached its simmer, pour half into the mixing bowl and whisk briskly. Add the remainder and repeat. Now return the mixture to the saucepan and cook, with constant whisking, over the gentlest possible heat; a heat diffuser would do good service here. When the sauce is thick enough to coat the back of a spoon, it's done. Strain into a clean bowl, leave to cool, then cover and refrigerate till needed.

You can make this stuff a few days in advance. You can flavour it further with spices, citrus, or ginger. You can even introduce a little alcohol if you like. Including brandy, for nostalgic appeal. But remember: the only place for brandy butter is in the bin, where it can do no harm.

INDEX